Grillin' in 'da  Tales from Life in Wisconsin

Wayne Larson

Grillin' in 'da Blizzard: Tales from Life in Wisconsin

by Wayne Larson

Paperback Edition

First Edition

ISBN: 9798344134918

Published by Jonathon Kelley

Printed in the United States of America

DEDICATION

To Karen, my North Star in every snowstorm.
For always keeping the coffee hot, the campfire burning, and my stories
mostly accurate.

And to the people of Wisconsin,
for teaching me that life's best moments are often the simplest:
a brat on the grill, a cold beer in hand, and good company to share it with.
This one's for all of you—

you betcha.

TABLE OF CONTENTS

ACKNOWLEDGMENTS

This book wouldn't exist without the support, stories, and occasional reality checks from the folks who have shared in my journey through the Great White Cheese State.

First and foremost, thank you to my wife, Karen. You've been my editor, my fact-checker, and my greatest adventure partner. You've patiently listened to my tales, endured my fish stories, and mastered the art of the polite eye-roll. Your warmth and practicality keep me grounded in every blizzard—both literal and metaphorical.

To my kids, who've grown up hearing my stories and occasionally believing them: thank you for the laughter, the memories, and the unspoken agreement not to roll your eyes (at least not too often) when I start another tall tale.

A huge thanks to the friends who have provided endless inspiration for these stories. Carl, you're a legend in your own right, and if this book ever takes off, I owe you a lifetime supply of brats. To everyone who's been a part of those Friday night fish fries, late-night card games, and campfire conversations—thanks for the laughter and the camaraderie. You've made the ordinary moments extraordinary.

To the good folks at the Pineville Press, thank you for taking a chance on a kid who thought he could turn his small-town observations into something worth reading. And to the many locals who shared their stories with me, thank you for trusting me to tell them. The characters in these pages may be fictional, but the spirit behind them is all of you.

To the state of Wisconsin itself, for the inspiration. You've given me the coldest winters, the warmest summers, and a community that knows how to embrace both. Whether it's on the ice, in the stands, or around the supper club table, you've shown me what it means to live life with resilience, humor, and an appreciation for the little things.

And finally, to my readers—whether you're lifelong Wisconsinites, transplanted Midwesterners, or curious outsiders—thank you for taking this journey with me. I hope these stories bring a smile to your face, a bit of warmth to your heart, and maybe even a craving for cheese curds.

Cheers to all of you, and remember: life's too short to skip the Friday night fish fry.

CHAPTER 1:
OPE! DIDN'T SEE YA THERE

If you're not familiar with the word "ope," you're probably not from Wisconsin—or the Midwest in general. "Ope!" is more than a word; it's an entire communication system. It's like a magic spell that makes awkward situations disappear. If you bump into someone at the grocery store, drop your keys in the Kwik Trip parking lot, or cut someone off at the four-way stop, just toss out an "Ope!" and you're forgiven. You're even friends now.

The first time I realized "Ope!" wasn't normal everywhere, I was on vacation in Florida. It was my first big trip out of the Midwest. You ever leave the Midwest and suddenly realize that people aren't as polite as you? It's a shock to the system. I was in line at a souvenir shop, looking at overpriced keychains shaped like flamingos, when I accidentally bumped into a woman in front of me. Instinctively, I let out a quick, "Ope, sorry!" She turned around and looked at me like I was having a stroke.

"You okay?" she asked, her Southern drawl dripping with suspicion.

"Oh, uh, yeah," I stammered, trying to explain. "I just... Ope... you know?"

She stared at me blankly. I panicked and decided it was safer to just leave the store. My wife asked me why I left so suddenly, and all I could say was, "They don't know what 'Ope!' means here." It was like a language barrier.

I was born and raised in the heart of Wisconsin. Growing up, I thought "Ope!" was just a part of being human. I assumed everybody said it. Like, why wouldn't you? It's the perfect word for when you don't know what else to say.

It's an apology, an acknowledgment, and a conversation starter all rolled into one. What's not to love?

The Swiss Army Knife of Words

Over the years, I've come to realize that "Ope!" is the Swiss army knife of the English language. You can use it in any situation, and it fits perfectly. You drop a plate of food—"Ope!" You're about to sneeze—"Ope!" You realize you left your phone in the car—"Ope!" It's versatile, efficient, and gets the job done without making a big fuss. It's the ultimate Midwestern tool.

The other day, I was at a Kwik Trip—where else?—grabbing some glazers and a gallon of milk. As I reached for the milk, another guy reached for the exact same gallon. We both paused, made eye contact, and simultaneously said, "Ope!" before breaking into polite laughter. It was like we'd rehearsed it. "Ope!" was our way of acknowledging that this situation was awkward, but we were both okay with it. We even ended up chatting about the Packers game the night before. Only in Wisconsin could an "Ope!" lead to a 10-minute conversation with a complete stranger.

That's the beauty of "Ope!" It's not just a word—it's an icebreaker. It's a way of saying, "Hey, we're all in this together, and I'm not mad about it."

Ope at Lambeau Field

My favorite "Ope!" story happened a few years ago at Lambeau Field. It was mid-December, and the Packers were playing the Bears. A classic rivalry, and the stakes were high. My buddy Ed and I had scored some tickets, and we were ready to brave the cold. Now, if you've never been to a Packers game in the dead of winter, you haven't experienced true Wisconsin. It's not just cold—it's "Why is my beard frozen?" cold. But that didn't stop anyone. We Wisconsinites are a hardy bunch, and we live for these moments.

As Ed and I made our way up to the bleachers, we were squeezed in tighter than bratwurst in a bun. I was trying to maneuver around a guy with a foam cheesehead the size of a small car when I slipped on the icy steps and stumbled forward, accidentally smacking another fan in the shoulder. Without missing a beat, we both shouted "Ope!" in unison. Then he turned to me and said, "All good, buddy. Go Pack Go!"

In that moment, I realized that "Ope!" wasn't just a way to apologize—it was a way to connect. It was like a secret handshake. It said, "We're both human, we both make mistakes, and we both love the Packers."

The rest of the game was a nail-biter. There were plenty more "Ope!" moments—like when the guy next to me accidentally spilled his beer on Ed's boots, or when the lady behind us dropped her hot dog and it rolled down two rows of seats. Each time, there was a collective "Ope!" and a chorus of chuckles. It was like Lambeau Field had its own soundtrack, and "Ope!" was the chorus.

The Family That Opes Together

Growing up, my family was big on "Ope!" My dad, a born-and-bred Wisconsinite, had perfected the art of the "Ope!" He could use it in any situation, and it always seemed to make things better. If he was telling a story and forgot what he was saying, he'd pause and say, "Ope, let me think for a sec." If he dropped his coffee mug, it was "Ope, guess I'll clean that up." Even when he was mad, it was never a full-on rant. Just an exasperated, "Ope, for Pete's sake!" and he'd move on.

My mom was the same way. She'd be in the middle of cooking dinner and suddenly remember she left the laundry in the dryer. She'd throw her hands up and say, "Ope! I forgot the clothes again." Then she'd laugh, like it was no big deal. And it wasn't. "Ope!" was our way of acknowledging that life is messy, and that's okay.

One Christmas, my little sister knocked over the tree while reaching for a candy cane. The whole thing came crashing down, ornaments shattering everywhere. She stood there, frozen in horror, while the rest of us just stared in disbelief. Then, out of the silence, my dad muttered, "Ope, that's not good." And just like that, the tension broke, and we all burst out laughing. Even my sister, who was on the verge of tears, couldn't help but giggle. "Ope!" saved Christmas.

Ope vs. the Rest of the World

Of course, not everyone understands the magic of "Ope!" I've got a cousin named Jerry who moved out to California a few years ago. He came back to visit last summer, and it was clear he'd lost touch with his Wisconsin roots. We were at a family cookout, and he dropped his phone on the ground. Instead of saying "Ope!" like a normal person, he muttered, "Darn it," and picked it up.

My uncle Larry just stared at him, like Jerry had committed some kind of unpardonable sin. "What's the matter with you, boy?" Larry said, shaking his head. "You forget how to Ope?"

Jerry looked confused. "How to what?"

3

"See?" Larry muttered to me. "That's what happens when you leave Wisconsin. You lose your Ope."

Jerry didn't even realize what he was missing, but we all felt sorry for him. He'd lost his connection to home. He was like a fish out of water, or worse—a Packers fan without a cheesehead.

I tried to explain "Ope!" to my friends in college, most of whom were from out of state. They didn't get it. They thought it was just a funny noise. One time, I bumped into a guy named Tom, who was from Texas, and I instinctively said, "Ope, sorry!"

He blinked at me. "Did you just say 'Ope'?"

"Yeah," I replied, like it was the most obvious thing in the world.

"What's that mean?" Tom asked, genuinely puzzled.

"It's like, you know… 'Oops' but… different," I stammered, struggling to put it into words.

Tom looked at me like I was an alien. "You Midwesterners are weird."

I wanted to argue, but deep down, I knew he was right. We are weird. But in the best possible way.

The Great "Ope!" Unifier

It took me a long time to realize that not everyone says "Ope!" And when I did, it only made me love it more. "Ope!" isn't just a word—it's a symbol of everything that makes Wisconsin, and the Midwest in general, special. It's humble, unassuming, and unpretentious. It's a little bit awkward, but in a charming way. It's an acknowledgment that life is full of small mistakes and unexpected moments, and that's what makes it interesting.

One of my favorite things about "Ope!" is that it brings people together. It's a reminder that we're all human, and we're all doing our best. Whether you're bumping into someone at Lambeau Field, reaching for the same gallon of milk at Kwik Trip, or accidentally knocking over the Christmas tree, "Ope!" is there to let you know that it's okay. We've all been there. We're all in this together.

So if you ever find yourself in Wisconsin—or anywhere in the Midwest, really—listen for the "Ope!" It's the sound of friendliness, humility, and good old-fashioned Midwestern charm. And if you hear someone say it, you'll know you're in good company.

And if you catch yourself saying it? Well, congratulations—you're officially one of us.

And there you have it: the power of "Ope!"—one small word with a big impact. It's more than a phrase; it's a way of life. So the next time you drop something, bump into someone, or just need a moment to gather your thoughts, remember to say "Ope!" It might just make everything a little bit better.

Wisconsinese Dictionary: Part 1
A Guide to Understanding the
True Language of Wisconsin

If you're planning to visit Wisconsin (or just trying to understand your Wisconsinite friends), you'll need to brush up on the local lingo. Here's a handy guide to translating common American English phrases into Wisconsinese—the unofficial language of the Great White Cheese State.

ENGLISH: "Excuse me"
WISCONSINEESE: "Ope, lemme just sneak past ya there"

Translation for when you need to pass by someone in a grocery store aisle or at a crowded Packers tailgate. No need for a formal "excuse me"—just throw in an "ope" and everyone's happy.

ENGLISH: "It's a bit chilly outside."
WISCONSINEESE: "It's not too bad, just throw on a hoodie."

A classic understatement, because unless it's below zero with a wind chill of -40, a hoodie will do the job.

ENGLISH: "Would you like something to drink?"
WISCONSINEESE: "You want a beer or a brandy Old Fashioned?"

The only two options that matter in Wisconsin. Asking if someone wants water or a soda? Amateurs.

ENGLISH:"I like cheese."
WISCONSINEESE: "I could marry a block of cheddar."

It's not a preference; it's a lifelong commitment. Don't be surprised if someone actually does this at the State Fair.

ENGLISH:"Let's go outside and enjoy the fresh air."
WISCONSINEESE:"Let's go sit on the deck, swat mosquitoes, and have a Leinenkugel's."

Because Wisconsin summers mean appreciating the outdoors with a side of bug spray and beer.

ENGLISH:"I'm not really into sports."
WISCONSINEESE: "I root for the Packers and whoever's playing the Bears."

You don't even have to watch football to know this rule. It's in the state constitution.

ENGLISH:"How's the weather?"
WISCONSINEESE: "You know, it's construction season."

In Wisconsin, the seasons are winter, still winter, road construction, and Packers preseason.

ENGLISH:"Would you like a glass of water?"
WISCONSINEESE: "Bubbler's over there."

When a Wisconsinite says "bubbler," they're not referring to a hot tub or a carbonation device—it's the water fountain.

ENGLISH:"Would you like something to eat?"
WISCONSINEESE: "How about some cheese curds?"

This question is mostly rhetorical because the answer should always be yes. And the follow-up question is, "Fresh or deep-fried?"

ENGLISH:"Can I help you find something?"
WISCONSINEESE:"You find everything you're lookin' for at Kwik Trip?"

The question you ask when someone's wandering aimlessly through the store. Because if they didn't find what they needed, they're clearly in the wrong place.

ENGLISH:"What's for dinner?"
WISCONSINEESE:"We're gonna hit the Friday night fish fry."

In Wisconsin, this isn't a suggestion—it's an obligation. If it's Friday and you're not having fried fish, people get concerned.

ENGLISH:"Do you want dessert?"
WISCONSINEESE:"We got kringle in the kitchen."

If you don't know what a kringle is, you'll be politely educated, and you'll probably leave with two or three slices for later.

ENGLISH:"It's great to see you!"
WISCONSINEESE: "How've you been since deer season?"

A common greeting in November. The more details you provide about your hunting stand, the closer you'll become as friends.

ENGLISH:"The snowstorm is really bad outside."
WISCONSINEESE: "Eh, just another Tuesday."

Anything less than a foot of snow is just a minor inconvenience. The plows are ready, the shovels are in the garage, and Kwik Trip is still open.

ENGLISH:"I'm sorry."
WISCONSINEESE:"Ope, my bad."

The more you say "ope," the more genuinely apologetic you sound. Bonus points if you add a quick chuckle to show you're not too worked up about it.

ENGLISH:"Let's have a nice family meal."
WISCONSINEESE: "We're goin' to the supper club."

The supper club is a Wisconsin institution where the meals are hearty, the Old Fashioneds are strong, and the waitstaff will remember your order from five years ago.

ENGLISH:"I'm feeling a bit under the weather."
WISCONSINEESE:"It's just a touch of cabin fever."

If you're feeling restless, it probably just means it's time to get outside for some ice fishing or snowmobiling.

ENGLISH:"I'm going to run some errands." \
WISCONSINEESE:"Gonna stop at Fleet Farm and Kwik Trip."

Wisconsinites know that if you're running errands, Fleet Farm and Kwik Trip are mandatory stops—no questions asked.

ENGLISH:"I'm really full."
WISCONSINEESE: "Okay, maybe just one more brat."

Because "full" is a state of mind, and there's always room for one more brat or cheese curd.

ENGLISH:"We'll be fine."
WISCONSINEESE: "We've got beer and cheese curds."

In Wisconsin, as long as you've got beer and cheese curds, you can weather any storm—literal or metaphorical.

Armed with this guide to Wisconsinese, you're ready to navigate the great state of Wisconsin like a local. Just remember: always be polite, keep the beer cold, and never forget to say "Ope!" when you accidentally bump into someone.

CHAPTER 2:
KWIK TRIP AND THE CIRCLE OF LIFE

In Wisconsin, we don't really have gas stations; we have Kwik Trip. And if you think a Kwik Trip is just a place to fill up your tank, you've clearly never been to one. Kwik Trip is more than a convenience store—it's a way of life. It's where you grab your morning coffee, catch up with neighbors, and discover random things you didn't know you needed. It's basically our version of Cheers, but with fewer barstools and more cheese curds.

A Morning at Kwik Trip

For me, a typical day starts with a stop at Kwik Trip. The sun is barely up, the roads are still covered in a thin layer of frost, and there I am, standing in line with the usual cast of characters: the farmer grabbing his morning coffee, the trucker stocking up on glazers, and the high school kid working the register who looks like he's already had a long day. We're all there for different reasons, but Kwik Trip is the great equalizer.

The first thing you need to know about Kwik Trip is that it's more than just gas and snacks. It's like a mini-grocery store, a bakery, and a community center all rolled into one. It's where you can fill up your tank, grab some bananas, and chat with the neighbor you haven't seen in weeks. And somehow, it all just makes sense.

I've got my Kwik Trip routine down to a science. First, I head to the bakery section to grab a glazer—or two, depending on how rough the week's been. Then it's over to the coffee bar for a cup of their signature House Blend. I don't know what they put in that coffee, but it's the closest thing to rocket fuel that's legal in Wisconsin. By the time I reach the checkout, I've usually added a carton of eggs, a loaf of bread, and maybe a brat for good measure. Because why not?

As I stand in line, I hear the usual conversations going on around me. The trucker is telling the cashier about the traffic on I-94, while the farmer is debating with a local about whether or not this winter is going to be worse than last year. Everyone's got an opinion, and everyone's got a story. It's like a live version of a local radio show, and the cast of characters is always changing.

One morning, I overheard a guy trying to explain to his buddy why Kwik Trip's bananas are superior to all other bananas. He had a whole theory worked out, complete with comparisons to the competition. "See, it's all about the freshness," he said, nodding wisely. "Kwik Trip gets their bananas straight from the source. None of that middleman nonsense."

Now, I don't know if that's true, but the conviction in his voice was enough to make me buy a bunch of bananas that day. And you know what? They were pretty good.

The Kwik Trip Glazers Conspiracy

Let's talk about glazers. If you're not from Wisconsin, you might not know what a glazer is. It's a donut, but not just any donut. It's the donut that all other donuts aspire to be. Soft, sweet, and glazed to perfection, a Kwik Trip glazer is like a little piece of heaven wrapped in wax paper.

There's a running joke in my town that if you want to know what's going on in the community, just hang out by the glazers at Kwik Trip. Everyone congregates there, and no one can resist reaching for one—especially when they're fresh out of the oven. It's like a gravitational pull that draws you in, whether you're there for gas or groceries.

I once asked a Kwik Trip employee what the secret was to making glazers so good. He just smiled and said, "It's all about the timing." He wouldn't give me any more details, and I couldn't tell if he was being serious or messing with me. Either way, I'm convinced there's a secret glazers recipe locked away somewhere in the Kwik Trip headquarters, guarded by a team of highly trained bakers. I wouldn't be surprised if they've got a whole underground network dedicated to glazer production.

Community at Kwik Trip

One of the things I love most about Kwik Trip is that it's a gathering place. It's where you run into people you haven't seen in a while, catch up on local news, and trade stories about everything from fishing trips to last night's

Packers game. It's like a small-town coffee shop, but with more hot dogs.

A couple of years ago, I ran into an old friend named Dave at Kwik Trip. I hadn't seen him in years, but there he was, standing in line with a coffee and a box of glazers. We started talking, and before we knew it, we'd been standing there for 20 minutes, holding up the line and catching up on everything from kids to work to our favorite fish fry spots. Finally, the cashier cleared her throat and said, "You boys gonna pay for those donuts, or are we having a reunion?"

We both laughed and apologized, but the truth is, that kind of thing happens all the time at Kwik Trip. It's not just a store; it's a community hub. It's where you bump into old friends, meet new ones, and find out what's going on in the world—all while grabbing a carton of milk and a bratwurst.

The Kwik Trip Impulse Buy

Here's the thing about Kwik Trip: you never leave with just what you came for. It doesn't matter if you're there for a gallon of milk or a loaf of bread—you're going to end up with a few extras. It's practically a law of nature.

One time, I went to Kwik Trip for a loaf of bread. That's it. Just bread. I even told myself, "Wayne, you're just getting bread. Don't get distracted." But then I saw the display of take-and-bake pizzas, and I thought, "Well, it's always good to have a pizza on hand, just in case." Then I passed the hot food section and spotted the mac and cheese, which looked way too good to pass up. By the time I reached the checkout, I had a loaf of bread, a pizza, a container of mac and cheese, and a bag of cheese curds. Because, you know, cheese curds.

I got home and my wife asked, "Did you get the bread?"

"Yep," I said proudly, holding up the loaf.

"And... all this other stuff?" she asked, raising an eyebrow.

"It's just... you know... essentials," I stammered.

She rolled her eyes, but deep down, I knew she was secretly grateful for the mac and cheese. It's a Wisconsin staple, after all.

The Kwik Trip Loyalty Program

Another thing you should know about Kwik Trip is their loyalty program. They've got this rewards card called "Kwik Rewards," and it's basically like winning the lottery for anyone who spends half their paycheck on glazers and take-and-bake pizzas.

The first time I signed up for Kwik Rewards, I was skeptical. I mean, how many rewards points could I really rack up from buying coffee and donuts? But then I started seeing the rewards roll in—free drinks, discounts on gas, and even a free glazer once in a while. It was like Christmas every month.

Now, I'm not saying I'm obsessed with earning rewards points, but let's just say I've been known to take the scenic route home so I can fill up at Kwik Trip and earn a few extra points. My wife says I'm like a kid collecting baseball cards, but I prefer to think of it as "strategic spending."

The best part is, you can track your rewards on the Kwik Trip app, which is basically my new favorite pastime. I check my points balance like it's my bank account, and every time I hit a new milestone, I feel like I've accomplished something great. "Honey, guess what?" I'll say, grinning from ear to ear. "I just earned a free coffee!"

She usually just rolls her eyes and says, "Congratulations, Wayne. You're a true champion."

The Kwik Trip Effect

There's something about Kwik Trip that just feels like home. Maybe it's the familiar layout, the friendly employees, or the smell of fresh-baked glazers. Whatever it is, Kwik Trip has become a part of my daily routine—and I'm not the only one. It's like a rite of passage for every Wisconsinite. You start with a coffee, move on to the breakfast sandwiches, and before you know it, you're picking up 10-pound bags of potatoes and debating the merits of take-and-bake pizza.

I once read that Kwik Trip was named the best gas station in America, and honestly, I wasn't surprised. It's not just a gas station—it's a lifestyle. And I'm not saying that as a joke. I genuinely believe that Kwik Trip has mastered the art of convenience in a way that other places can only dream of.

I've got a cousin from Illinois (we don't hold it against him), and whenever he visits, he's always amazed by Kwik Trip. "You guys have fresh produce in your gas stations?" he asks, like we've discovered the secret to life.

"Of course," I reply. "What kind of gas station doesn't sell bananas?"

The last time he visited, he bought a whole bag of glazers to take back home with him. "They don't have these in Illinois," he said wistfully.

"Good," I replied. "That's how we keep our edge."

The Secret Life of Kwik Trip Employees

Now, I've spent enough time at Kwik Trip to get to know some of the employees. And let me tell you, they've got some stories. One guy, named Randy, has worked at Kwik Trip for over 15 years. He's seen it all—late-night shenanigans, road-weary travelers, and more arguments over cheese curds than he cares to count.

One day, I asked Randy what the weirdest thing he'd ever seen was. He thought for a moment and said, "Well, there was that time a guy tried to grill brats in the parking lot."

"What?" I laughed. "Why?"

"I don't know," Randy shrugged. "He said he couldn't wait to get home, and he had the grill in his truck, so he figured why not?"

That's the kind of place Kwik Trip is. It's a place where people feel comfortable enough to fire up a grill in the parking lot. And honestly? I respect that kind of dedication.

The Eulogy for a Closed Kwik Trip

There was a Kwik Trip in my hometown that shut down a few years ago. It was a sad day for all of us. We'd been going there for as long as I could remember, and it felt like losing a piece of history. When word got out that the store was closing, there was an outpouring of emotion on social media. People shared memories of grabbing glazers before school, filling up the tank before family road trips, and meeting friends for coffee on Sunday mornings.

A group of locals even organized a "farewell party" in the parking lot. They brought lawn chairs, coolers, and, of course, grills. It was like a mini-festival, complete with bratwursts and impromptu speeches about the impact that Kwik Trip had on our lives. One guy stood up and said, "This place got me through college. I wouldn't have made it without those glazers and cheap coffee."

Another woman wiped away a tear and said, "Kwik Trip was where my husband proposed to me. Right by the ice cream freezer."

It was both hilarious and heartwarming, and it made me realize just how much Kwik Trip meant to all of us. It wasn't just a store—it was a part of our lives.

Why We Love Kwik Trip

In the end, I think the reason we all love Kwik Trip so much is because it represents everything that's great about Wisconsin. It's friendly, unpretentious, and full of good food. It's a place where you can grab a brat, chat with your neighbors, and pick up a gallon of milk on your way home. It's the little things that make life in Wisconsin so special, and Kwik Trip is one of those little things.

So the next time you find yourself at Kwik Trip, take a moment to appreciate the simple joys of life—a fresh glazer, a hot cup of coffee, and a chat with an old friend. And if you happen to bump into someone, don't forget to say "Ope!"

Here's a list of Wisconsin facts my uncles told me about at lunch after Sunday church:

Cheesehead Olympics:
Every year, Wisconsin hosts the Cheesehead Olympics, where athletes compete in events like cheese rolling, cow tipping, and bratwurst tossing.

Sconnie Dialect (Wisconsineese):
The official state language is a blend of English and "Sconnie," which includes phrases like "Oh, fer cryin' out loud!" and "You betcha!"

Badger Mascot Secret:
The University of Wisconsin's mascot, Bucky Badger, is rumored to have a secret life as a cheese sculptor during the off-season.

World's Largest Pretzel:
Wisconsin is home to the world's largest pretzel, which is so big it has its own zip code and is affectionately named "Pretzel Pete."

Winter Weather Contest:
Every winter, towns compete to see who can build the tallest snowman. The reigning champion is said to have created one tall enough to touch the clouds.

Milwaukee's Water Skiing Penguins:
Legend has it that a group of penguins escaped from a nearby zoo and now performs synchronized water skiing shows on Lake Michigan.

The Great Sauerkraut Debate:
Wisconsin hosts an annual festival dedicated to sauerkraut, where locals argue passionately about the best toppings—everything from cheese curds to wildflowers!

Fondue Fountains in the Capitol:
The Wisconsin State Capitol is said to have a secret fondue fountain hidden in its basement, serving only the finest cheddar.

Giant Mosquitoes:
Wisconsin mosquitoes are so large they have their own state park, where visitors can take guided tours to spot the elusive "Wisconsin Winged Behemoths."

Badger-Saving Superheroes:
A group of local "badger superheroes" roams the state, rescuing lost badgers and promoting good cheese etiquette.

Ope, now don't go quoting me on this, I'm just tellin' ya what I herd. My Uncles have been know to spin a tale or two, 'specially Uncle Frank. But, now you know what I know.

Chapter 3:
The Art of Grilling in a Blizzard

In Wisconsin, we have a saying: "There's no such thing as bad weather, just bad planning." It's the kind of wisdom that gets passed down from generation to generation, along with family recipes for brats and tips on snowblower maintenance. For most people, grilling is a fair-weather activity. But here in Wisconsin, it's a year-round sport. Rain, sleet, snow, or shine, we grill. And if you think that sounds insane, then you've clearly never tasted a brat cooked over charcoal in the middle of a blizzard.

A Cookout for the Ages

One winter, we got hit with a snowstorm so fierce that even the meteorologists were running out of ways to describe it. "Polar vortex," "snowpocalypse," and "Siberian express" were just a few of the terms they threw around. But for my buddy Carl, it was just another excuse to fire up the grill.

Carl's the kind of guy who's got grilling in his blood. If you looked at his family tree, I'm pretty sure you'd find a Weber Grill somewhere in the roots. He's the kind of guy who believes there's no problem that can't be solved with a brat and a cold beer. So when Carl invited us over for a cookout in the middle of the storm, none of us were surprised. In fact, we were excited.

The snow was coming down sideways as we pulled up to Carl's place. His driveway looked more like a luge track, and his yard was buried under three feet of snow. But there, in the middle of it all, was Carl, standing by his grill with an umbrella in one hand and a pair of tongs in the other.

"Come on in, boys!" Carl shouted, waving us over. "The brats are almost done!"

We made our way through the snow, slipping and sliding like penguins on ice. Carl had set up a makeshift grilling station next to his garage, with the grill wedged between two snowbanks for extra wind protection. He'd even cleared out a little patch of ground for us to stand on, using his snowblower to create a path that looked like a miniature snow canyon.

"Cold enough for ya?" Carl asked, grinning from ear to ear.

"Oh, it's fine," I replied, trying to sound nonchalant as my eyelashes froze together.

Grilling Techniques for Extreme Weather

Grilling in a blizzard isn't as simple as throwing some brats on the grill and hoping for the best. It requires strategy, preparation, and a healthy disregard for common sense. Over the years, I've picked up a few tips and tricks for grilling in extreme weather—most of them learned through trial and error.

The first rule of blizzard grilling is to keep the grill hot. Cold winds can sap the heat from your grill faster than you can say "charcoal chimney," so it's important to start with a roaring fire. I once saw Carl light his grill using a blowtorch, and while it seemed excessive at the time, I have to admit that it got the job done.

The second rule is to embrace the elements. If you're worried about getting snow on your food, then blizzard grilling probably isn't for you. Personally, I like to think of a little snow on my brat as an extra seasoning. It adds character.

Finally, the third rule is to always have a backup plan. You never know when a gust of wind is going to knock over your grill or send your umbrella flying across the yard. That's why I always keep a propane grill on standby, just in case the charcoal doesn't cooperate. It's not as authentic, but sometimes you've got to compromise for the sake of dinner.

The Great Grill-Off

Grilling isn't just a way to cook food—it's a competitive sport. In my neighborhood, we've got an annual tradition called the Great Grill-Off, where everyone brings their best brats, burgers, and sausages to compete for the title of "Best Griller on the Block." It's a friendly competition, but make no mistake—it's intense.

One year, Carl decided to enter the Grill-Off with a secret weapon: his famous "Polar Brats," which he claimed were marinated in a special blend of beer, spices, and "a little bit of magic." I don't know what was in that marinade, but the brats were so good that they practically melted in your mouth.

Not to be outdone, I entered the competition with my own creation: the "Blizzard Burger"—a half-pound patty topped with melted cheese curds and a drizzle of beer cheese sauce. It was a heart attack on a bun, but that's what makes it so delicious.

The judges for the Grill-Off are a panel of local "experts," which usually includes our neighbor Marge, who once won a blue ribbon at the county fair for her potato salad, and old man Jenkins, who claims to have invented the reverse sear. Their judging criteria include taste, creativity, and "grillmanship," which is basically a fancy way of saying "how much you look like you know what you're doing."

Carl ended up winning that year with his Polar Brats, but I came in a close second with my Blizzard Burger. I didn't mind losing, though, because in the end, we all got to eat a lot of good food and drink a lot of beer. And that's what really matters.

What's on the Grill?

If you ask a Wisconsinite what they like to grill, you'll get a wide range of answers. Brats are a given, of course, but there's a lot more to Wisconsin grilling than just sausage.

Venison steaks are a popular choice, especially during hunting season. I've got a neighbor named Jim who's an avid hunter, and every year he gives me a couple of venison steaks as a "thank you" for letting him borrow my snowblower. I've tried grilling them a few different ways, but my favorite method is to marinate them in Worcestershire sauce and garlic before searing them over high heat. They're lean and flavorful, with just a hint of smokiness from the grill.

Fish is another common item on the Wisconsin grill, especially walleye. There's nothing quite like grilling a fresh-caught walleye over an open flame, with a little bit of lemon and butter. I've got a buddy named Steve who insists on grilling his walleye with the skin on, saying it adds flavor and helps keep the fish from falling apart. I'm not sure if that's true, but it sounds good, so I go along with it.

And then there are the more unconventional choices. One time, Carl decided to try grilling cheese curds. I told him he was crazy, but he insisted that it would work. He wrapped the curds in foil and set them on the grill, hoping they'd melt just enough to get gooey without turning into a puddle of cheese.

Well, they didn't exactly hold their shape, but the result was a gooey, cheesy mess that we ended up eating with forks. It wasn't pretty, but it was delicious, and that's what counts.

Grilling Disasters

Of course, not every grilling adventure goes according to plan. Over the years, I've had my fair share of grilling disasters, and I've learned that sometimes you just have to roll with the punches.

One winter, I decided to grill a batch of brats during a particularly nasty snowstorm. I'd shoveled a path to the grill and got the coals nice and hot, but just as I was about to put the brats on, a gust of wind blew the lid off the grill and sent it tumbling across the yard. I chased after it, slipping and sliding in the snow, while the coals slowly died out in the wind.

By the time I got the lid back on the grill, the coals were barely warm, and the brats were still raw. My wife came outside to see what was taking so long, and all I could do was shrug and say, "Well, it seemed like a good idea at the time."

Then there was the time my neighbor Mike tried to grill in his garage during a rainstorm. He propped the garage door open for ventilation and set up his grill just inside the doorway. Everything was going fine until the smoke alarm went off, and Mike's wife came running out, yelling, "Are you trying to burn down the house?!"

Mike ended up finishing his burgers in the oven that night, but he's still convinced that grilling in the garage is a viable option.

Why We Grill in Any Weather

So why do we Wisconsinites insist on grilling, no matter the weather? I think it's partly about resilience. We like to prove that we're tough enough to handle whatever Mother Nature throws at us. It's also about optimism. Even in the dead of winter, when the days are short and the nights are freezing, there's something hopeful about firing up the grill and enjoying a taste of summer.

But more than anything, I think it's about community. Grilling brings people together, whether it's for a neighborhood cookout, a family reunion, or a spur-of-the-moment dinner with friends. It's a way of celebrating life's little moments, even when the world outside is cold and unforgiving.

When we grill in a blizzard, we're not just cooking food—we're making memories. We're sharing stories, laughing at our mistakes, and finding joy in the simple act of being together. And in a world that's often chaotic and unpredictable, there's something comforting about that.

The Cookout in the Blizzard: A Perfect End

Back at Carl's house, the cookout in the blizzard was in full swing. We huddled around the grill, braving the cold as Carl flipped the brats with expert precision. The snow was still coming down, but we didn't mind. We had warm food, cold beer, and good company. What more could we ask for?

As we ate, we swapped stories about past cookouts, shared tips on grilling techniques, and laughed about the time Carl tried to make grilled cheese curds. It was one of those moments that felt both completely ordinary and wonderfully special at the same time.

By the time the snow finally let up, we were full, happy, and thoroughly chilled to the bone. But as I stood there, surrounded by friends and the smell of grilled brats, I couldn't help but feel a sense of pride. We'd faced the elements, embraced the cold, and come out on the other side with full bellies and warm hearts.

And that, my friends, is the art of grilling in a blizzard.

Tips and Tricks for Grillin' in a Blizzard: A Survival Guide

1 - Start with a Shovel, Not Tongs

Before you even think about firing up the grill, clear a path to it! A snow-covered grill is just a bench. Make sure to shovel a good-sized area around the grill to avoid any accidental face-plants into snowdrifts while flipping burgers.

2 - Preheat? More Like Defrost!

If your grill hasn't seen daylight since last summer, it probably needs a little TLC. Give it a good scrape to knock off any ice, snow, or those leftover brats from the Fourth of July. Preheat that baby a bit longer than usual to get the ice and snow fully out of the equation.

3 - Brats Stay Cozy; Keep the Lid Closed

You might be tempted to keep checking on your brats, but every time you lift the lid, you're letting out precious heat and letting in an Arctic blast. Remember: Grilling in the snow is like dealing with a stubborn teen—if you hover, nothing gets done!

4 - Dress Like You're Ice Fishing, Not Beach Grilling

Wearing shorts and flip-flops in a blizzard may earn you street cred in some circles, but it won't help you handle a hot grill in freezing temperatures. Bundle up, but remember that a bulky coat and oven mitts can lead to dropped brats. You don't want to be that person who needs to fish a brat out of a snowbank.

5 - Beer: For Sipping, Not Extinguishing Flames

We know that the snow is nature's cooler, but don't get overconfident. Keep the beer in hand for drinking, not for dousing unexpected flare-ups. Your taste buds will thank you, and the fire department will appreciate it.

6 - Check the Wind Chill Factor on Your Propane

If it's so cold that your breath freezes mid-air, your propane might be suffering too. A half-empty tank could leave you high and dry—or, worse, with a bunch of half-cooked steaks. Keep a spare tank handy, just in case Old Man Winter decides to turn your BBQ into a popsicle stand.

7 - Lean into the 'Wisconsin Sauna' Technique

When it's snowing hard, that grill smoke and steam combo can create your very own backyard sauna. Just lean in, and take a deep breath of that brat-infused mist. Who needs a fancy spa day when you've got grill steam therapy?

8 - Keep One Hand on the Tongs, One on the Hot Toddy

Grilling in the snow is a two-handed operation. You've got to flip those brats with precision while keeping your other hand occupied with a hot drink for morale purposes. It's basic Wisconsin physics: hot beverage = warm grillmaster.

9 - A Snowbank Is Mother Nature's Cooler

When space gets tight on the grill, no worries—just stick your beer or brats in the nearest snowbank. Nature's cooler works faster than anything from your fridge, and you won't need to dig out the cooler from the garage.

10 - Practice the 'Midwestern Ope' Maneuver

If you drop a brat, don't panic—just give it a quick "Ope!" and scoop it up in one smooth motion. A little snow never hurt anyone. Brush it off, toss it back on the grill, and no one's the wiser. (That's what extra char is for!)

11 - Don't Underestimate the Power of Duct Tape

If the wind's howling and your grill cover starts flapping, don't spend an hour fighting it. Grab some good ol' duct tape and secure it. Duct tape is the unofficial state adhesive, and in blizzard conditions, it's worth its weight in gold.

12 - Brat Thermometers Are for Summer, Use Your Gut

In a blizzard, you don't have time for fancy tools and thermometers. Trust your gut, and give each brat a quick poke. If it feels hot enough and has a

good char, it's done. Plus, you're cold—don't overthink it.

13 - Build a Snow-Windshield

The ultimate pro move: use the snow around you to build a little wall to block the wind. Not only does it keep your grill going strong, but it also doubles as a fortress for keeping out nosy neighbors or in-laws.

14 - Be Ready with a 'Hotdish' Backup Plan

If all else fails and the wind wins, or the snow decides to have a say in your grilling, it's always smart to have a backup plan. Nothing says "Grillin' in Wisconsin" like Plan B hotdish on the stove.

15 - Have a Cheese Melt Option Ready

This isn't just about brats or burgers. Wisconsin grilling in winter isn't complete without tossing a cast-iron skillet on the grill and melting some local cheddar. Just toss in some cheese curds, let them get gooey, and serve with pride.

16 - Turn Off the Grill, Not the Party

When you've successfully braved the blizzard, cooked those brats, and polished off your last beer, remember: the end of grilling isn't the end of the fun. Invite everyone inside, warm up with a game of Euchre, and laugh about the fact that you willingly grilled in a snowstorm.

Grillin' in the snow isn't just an activity—it's a state of mind. It's a declaration that no matter what Mother Nature throws at us, we Wisconsinites will always find a way to enjoy a brat and a beer. So get out there, fire up that grill, and show winter who's boss. You got this. Ope!

CHAPTER 4:
THE FISH FRY FRIDAYS THAT ALMOST ENDED A FRIENDSHIP

If you ever want to see a true Wisconsinite get passionate, don't ask them about politics or sports. No, the real heart and soul of Wisconsin lies in one simple question: "Where's the best fish fry around here?" Ask that in any small town, and you'll start a debate that could outlast a Lambeau Field overtime game. For us, Friday night fish fry isn't just a meal—it's practically a religion.

There's something sacred about walking into a Wisconsin tavern on a Friday evening, the air thick with the smell of fried cod, walleye, or perch. The tables are filled with families, regulars, and first-timers who have no idea they're about to experience culinary enlightenment. The bartender, who's been there longer than you've been alive, mixes brandy Old Fashioneds with the grace of a concert pianist, and the hush of conversation is punctuated by the occasional yell of "Bingo!" from the back room. It's a scene so quintessentially Wisconsin that it ought to be printed on postcards.

The Great Fish Fry Debate

Now, in Wisconsin, we take our fish fries seriously. There are two things that make or break a fish fry: the fish and the tartar sauce. Some folks are partial to cod, others prefer perch or walleye. Then there's the matter of sides: potato pancakes or French fries? Coleslaw or baked beans? And don't even get me started on the rye bread vs. dinner roll debate. People have ended friendships over less.

Speaking of friendships, I once had a near-falling out with my good buddy Jim over a fish fry debate. It all started innocently enough. We were sitting in our favorite tavern, The Rusty Reel, enjoying a few beers when Jim said, "You know, the fish here is good, but it's not as good as Al's Lakeview."

Now, I've got nothing against Al's Lakeview. It's a decent place, and the view of the lake is nice, but their fish fry? Let's just say it's fine. Not great, not terrible, just fine. So when Jim compared it to The Rusty Reel, which in my opinion serves the best fish in town, I had to speak up.

"You're out of your mind," I said, shaking my head. "The fish here is way better. It's got the perfect ratio of batter to fish, and their tartar sauce is homemade."

Jim rolled his eyes. "Homemade doesn't mean better," he shot back. "Al's tartar sauce comes in those little packets, and you know what? It's just as good."

I couldn't believe what I was hearing. Packet tartar sauce? Better than homemade? That was blasphemy. I took a deep breath, trying to keep my cool. "Jim, listen," I said, leaning in. "You're comparing packet sauce to the real deal. That's like saying the Packers are just as good as the Bears."

Jim's face turned red. "I never said that!" he yelled, attracting the attention of the bartender, who raised an eyebrow in our direction.

"Okay, okay," I said, trying to de-escalate the situation. "Let's settle this like gentlemen. How about a cook-off? We'll each make our own fish fry, and we'll let the neighbors decide whose is better."

Jim thought about it for a moment and then nodded. "You're on," he said, extending his hand. We shook on it, and the Great Fish Fry Cook-Off was officially underway.

The Fish Fry Cook-Off

The day of the cook-off, I woke up early and got to work. I had a plan: a perfectly seasoned beer batter, hand-cut fries, homemade coleslaw, and—of course—my famous tartar sauce. I wasn't going to take any chances, so I spent all morning perfecting the recipe and practicing my fry technique. My wife thought I was crazy, but I knew this was a matter of pride.

Jim, meanwhile, took a more laid-back approach. He showed up at my house with a cooler full of frozen fish fillets and a bag of store-bought fries. I knew I had the upper hand, but I wasn't about to let my guard down. Jim's a crafty guy, and I wasn't sure what tricks he had up his sleeve.

We set up our grills in the backyard and got to work. The air was filled with the smell of hot oil and sizzling fish, and soon, a crowd of curious neighbors had gathered to watch the showdown. Marge from down the street brought her famous potato salad, and old man Jenkins—who'd been the self-proclaimed fish fry expert for as long as anyone could remember—pulled up a lawn chair and cracked open a beer.

As we cooked, Jim and I traded good-natured jabs. "You sure you don't want to use some real fish?" I asked, pointing to his frozen fillets.

Jim just grinned. "It's not the fish, Wayne. It's the frying technique that matters."

When everything was ready, we set up a tasting station and invited the neighbors to try our creations. They sampled the fish, debated the merits of each tartar sauce, and argued over whether fries or potato pancakes were the superior side. It was like a town hall meeting, but with more food and fewer arguments about taxes.

The Judging

The moment of truth came when old man Jenkins approached the tasting station. He took his time sampling each fish, nodding thoughtfully as he chewed. When he was finished, he cleared his throat and addressed the crowd.

"Well," he said, "I gotta say, both these fish fries are pretty darn good. But if I had to choose, I'd go with…" He paused for dramatic effect, and Jim and I held our breath. "…Wayne's fish."

The crowd erupted in applause, and I couldn't help but grin. Jim looked disappointed, but he took it in stride. "Good job, Wayne," he said, giving me a nod. "You earned it."

As the crowd dispersed, Marge leaned over and whispered, "You know, Wayne, your fish is good, but Jim's tartar sauce is still my favorite."

I laughed and shook my head. "There's no winning with you, Marge."

A Statewide Tradition

The truth is, no matter where you go in Wisconsin, you'll find someone who claims to know the best fish fry. And you know what? They're probably right. Because the best fish fry isn't just about the food—it's about the experience. It's about gathering with friends and family, enjoying a cold beer, and swapping stories about the big catch you almost got last summer.

Some of the best fish fries I've ever had weren't at fancy restaurants—they were in church basements and VFW halls, where the fish is served on paper plates and the tartar sauce is made by someone's grandma. It's not about perfection; it's about tradition. And that's what makes it special.

Every small town has its own version of the perfect fish fry. Some places serve perch with potato pancakes, while others stick to cod with French fries. Some folks like their coleslaw creamy, while others prefer it tangy. But no matter where you go, the one thing you can always count on is a warm welcome and a cold drink.

Supper Clubs and Rituals

Now, if you want to take your fish fry experience to the next level, you've got to visit a supper club. These places are like time capsules from the 1960s, with dim lighting, wood-paneled walls, and plush booths that make you feel like you're stepping into a scene from Mad Men. The waitstaff wear matching uniforms, and the menu is full of classic dishes like prime rib, shrimp scampi, and—of course—Friday night fish fry.

The supper club fish fry is a thing of beauty. It usually starts with a relish tray, complete with pickled beets, carrot sticks, and a mysterious cheese spread that may or may not be from the last century. Then comes the main event: a heaping plate of fried fish, potato pancakes, coleslaw, and rye bread. If you're feeling fancy, you can wash it all down with a brandy Old Fashioned, which is practically a requirement at any self-respecting supper club.

I once took a friend from out of state to a supper club, and he was completely overwhelmed. "What is this place?" he asked, wide-eyed as the waitress brought over a relish tray.

"Welcome to heaven," I replied.

WAYNE LARSON

Fish Fry Friendships

In the end, the Great Fish Fry Cook-Off didn't end our friendship—it

made it stronger. Jim and I still debate the best place to get fish, but now we do it with a sense of humor and a shared appreciation for the tradition. We've both come to realize that the best fish fry isn't necessarily about who's got the crispiest batter or the tastiest tartar sauce. It's about the memories you make and the people you share it with.

Every time I sit down to a fish fry, I'm reminded of the countless Fridays I've spent with friends and family, gathered around a table filled with food, laughter, and the occasional argument about whether potato pancakes are better than fries. It's a ritual that connects us to our past, our present, and each other.

So the next time you find yourself in Wisconsin on a Friday night, do yourself a favor: find a local tavern, order the fish fry, and strike up a conversation with the folks sitting next to you. You might just make a new friend—or start a friendly feud over the best tartar sauce. Either way, you're in for a good time.

Classic Wisconsin Friday Night Fish Fry Recipe
(With a Side of Wisconsin Humor)

When it comes to a classic Wisconsin fish fry, simplicity, tradition, and a little bit of Midwestern wit are key. This recipe is designed to recreate the flavors and experience of a true Wisconsin supper club fish fry, complete with golden-fried fish, crispy potato pancakes, tangy coleslaw, and that essential side of rye bread and butter. Grab a cold beer, crank up the polka music, and let's get frying!

Ingredients:

For the Fish:

- ❖ 2 pounds fresh white fish fillets (walleye, perch, or cod—anything you can pull out of Lake Mendota without making the DNR suspicious)
- ❖ 1 cup all-purpose flour (or as we call it, "breading magic")
- ❖ 1 cup cornmeal
- ❖ 1 tablespoon garlic powder (because vampires aren't welcome at this fish fry)
- ❖ 1 teaspoon smoked paprika (for that hint of "mystery")
- ❖ 1 teaspoon salt (to season those fishies just right)
- ❖ 1/2 teaspoon black pepper
- ❖ 1 teaspoon Old Bay seasoning (optional, but it's a good insurance policy against anyone calling you a "Minnesota Nice" cook)
- ❖ 2 large eggs (preferably from a friend's backyard chickens)
- ❖ 1 cup beer (preferably a Wisconsin beer like Spotted Cow or Miller High Life—just don't use the last one, or you'll have an angry crowd)
- ❖ Vegetable oil, for frying (save the bacon grease for breakfast tomorrow)

For the Potato Pancakes:

- ❖ 3 medium russet potatoes, peeled and grated (or stolen from a relative's basement stash)
- ❖ 1 small onion, grated (because even your onions should have a little cry in them about this weather)
- ❖ 1 large egg
- ❖ 1/4 cup flour
- ❖ Salt and pepper, to taste
- ❖ 1/2 teaspoon baking powder

❖ Vegetable oil or butter, for frying (we won't judge if you use a mix—this is Wisconsin after all)

For the Coleslaw:

❖ 4 cups shredded cabbage (preferably hand-chopped while complaining about the Packers' last season)
❖ 1 cup shredded carrots
❖ 1/2 cup mayonnaise (yes, it's an essential food group)
❖ 2 tablespoons apple cider vinegar
❖ 2 tablespoons sugar (to sweeten up that Midwest "tang")
❖ 1/2 teaspoon celery seed (because if there's not celery seed, did you even make coleslaw?)
❖ Salt and pepper, to taste

For Serving:

❖ Rye bread and butter (the true Wisconsin way—none of that fancy French baguette nonsense)
❖ Lemon wedges
❖ Tartar sauce (store-bought, homemade, or borrowed from your in-law's fridge)

Directions:

Step 1: Prepare the Fish Batter

Mix the dry ingredients: In a shallow dish, combine the flour, cornmeal, garlic powder, smoked paprika, salt, pepper, and Old Bay seasoning. This is your "magic coating," and no one needs to know you eyeballed the measurements like a seasoned supper club chef.

Make the batter: In a medium bowl, whisk together the eggs and beer until combined. The batter should be slightly thick and bubbly—kind of like Uncle Jim after a Packers game.

Dip the fish: Pat the fish fillets dry with a paper towel. Lightly dredge each fillet in the flour mixture, shaking off any excess. Then, dip each fillet into the beer batter, making sure it's fully coated. Let any excess batter drip off, but remember: don't be stingy—this isn't Lent.

Step 2: Fry the Fish

Heat the oil: In a large, heavy-bottomed skillet or deep fryer, heat about an inch of vegetable oil to 350°F. (If you're not sure it's ready, just ask your nearest elderly relative—they'll give it a sniff and say, "Yup, good enough.")

Fry the fish: Carefully lower the battered fillets into the hot oil, a few at a time. Fry until golden brown and crispy, about 3-4 minutes per side. Don't overcrowd the pan, or the fish will get a little claustrophobic and start losing its crisp.

Drain and keep warm: Once the fish is golden and cooked through, transfer it to a paper towel-lined plate to drain excess oil. Sprinkle with a little salt while hot and keep it warm in a low oven until ready to serve. You can set your oven to Wisconsin standard low, which is "leave the door open for the cat to sleep by."

Step 3: Make the Potato Pancakes

Grate the potatoes and onion: After grating, use a clean kitchen towel to wring out as much moisture as possible from the grated potatoes and onions. This step is crucial for achieving crispy pancakes, or as my Aunt Marge says, "If they're soggy, the Vikings must have made 'em."

Mix the batter: In a bowl, combine the grated potatoes, grated onion, egg, flour, baking powder, salt, and pepper. Mix until well combined.

Fry the pancakes: In a skillet, heat a tablespoon of vegetable oil or butter over medium heat. Drop a spoonful of the potato mixture into the hot skillet, flattening it slightly with the back of the spoon. Cook until golden brown and crispy on both sides, about 3-4 minutes per side. Keep warm in the oven—if you're lucky, the cat won't eat them.

Step 4: Prepare the Coleslaw

Combine the veggies: In a large bowl, toss together the shredded cabbage and shredded carrots. Pro tip: keep a portion of cabbage raw to remind you of that time you got caught outside without a hat.

Make the dressing: In a small bowl, whisk together the mayonnaise, apple cider vinegar, sugar, celery seed, salt, and pepper until smooth. Just like the Packers' O-line, consistency is key here.

Mix it all together: Pour the dressing over the cabbage mixture and toss until well coated. Cover and refrigerate until ready to serve. You want the slaw chilled, not "Wisconsin winter windshield" frozen.

Step 5: Serve It Up, Wisconsin Style

Arrange the fish: Place the crispy fried fish on a platter, garnished with lemon wedges for that "fancy supper club" look.

Serve the sides: Arrange the potato pancakes, coleslaw, and rye bread with butter on separate plates. For authenticity, slice the rye bread unevenly like your Uncle Dave does after two Old Fashioneds.

Add the finishing touches: Serve with tartar sauce on the side for dipping, and don't forget the beer! A Wisconsin fish fry isn't complete without a cold brew to wash it all down. If anyone tries to drink water with this meal, kindly direct them to the cheese plate until they rethink their life choices.

Tips for an Authentic Wisconsin Experience:

- ❖ Use local fish: If you can, use local walleye or perch for that authentic touch. If you didn't catch it yourself, it's still okay—as long as you pretend you did.
- ❖ Keep the beer cold: It goes without saying, but if your beer isn't cold, you're not doing it right. The snowbank outside makes a great cooler—just remember which one your beers are in, or you'll be doing the "snow shuffle."
- ❖ Play polka music in the background: If someone in the family doesn't start unconsciously tapping their foot, you're playing it too soft.
- ❖ Serve with a smile: The key to a great Wisconsin fish fry is sharing it with friends, neighbors, and any in-laws who promise not to mention the Packers' last playoff game.
- ❖ Enjoy!

Congratulations—you've just created a classic Wisconsin fish fry, complete with all the traditions, flavors, and a few laughs. Whether you're a lifelong Wisconsinite or just someone looking to experience the magic of the Great White Cheese State, remember: the best fish fry isn't just about the food—it's about the company, the conversation, and the chance to relax and say, "Ope, pass me another brat."

Chapter 5:
A Beginner's Guide to Navigating Road Construction Season

If you've ever been to Wisconsin, you've probably heard the joke: "In Wisconsin, we have two seasons—winter and road construction." And like most jokes rooted in painful truth, it's funny because it's true. You know it's road construction season in Wisconsin when the snow finally melts, the robins start singing, and suddenly every road you need to drive on is covered in a sea of orange barrels and "Detour" signs.

For us Wisconsinites, road construction isn't just a minor inconvenience—it's a way of life. Navigating road construction season requires patience, planning, and a willingness to accept the fact that you're going to be late for everything. I've spent most of my life dodging potholes, following confusing detours, and trying to decipher road signs that look like they were drawn by someone playing Pictionary after a few Old Fashioneds. Over the years, I've picked up a few tricks for surviving the chaos, and I'm here to share them with you.

The Orange Barrel Obstacle Course

There's nothing quite like the sight of orange barrels lining a two-lane highway, creating a labyrinth that forces you to weave in and out like you're in a game of Mario Kart. One wrong move, and you're either stuck in a traffic jam or accidentally driving through someone's front yard. It's enough to make you question your sanity—or at least your decision to leave the house in the first place.

One summer, I was driving through Milwaukee, trying to get to a Brewers game. I had my route all planned out, with plenty of time to spare. But as soon as I got onto the highway, I was met with a wall of orange barrels and a flashing sign that said "ROAD CLOSED AHEAD. FOLLOW DETOUR." I sighed, turned on my blinker, and dutifully followed the detour.

That detour led me through half of Milwaukee and most of the surrounding suburbs. At one point, I ended up in a neighborhood that looked like it hadn't seen a car since the '90s. I drove past three lemonade stands, a guy mowing his lawn in a speedo, and a goat tied to a tree (don't ask). By the time I got back on the highway, I'd missed the first three innings of the game, and I was too tired to care.

I'd like to say that experience taught me to be more prepared, but let's be honest—there's no preparing for road construction in Wisconsin. You just have to accept it, embrace it, and hope you don't end up in Illinois by mistake.

Small Town Shenanigans

While city construction can be a nightmare, small town construction is a whole different beast. In small towns, road construction season is practically a spectator sport. The entire town gathers to watch the road crew tear up Main Street, like it's the biggest event of the year. It's not unusual to see people sitting in lawn chairs, sipping lemonade, and commenting on the workers' progress like they're watching a Packers game.

In my hometown, the road crew once redirected traffic through a cow pasture. I'm not kidding. They tore up Main Street to fix a sewer line, and the only way to get from one side of town to the other was to cut through old man Johnson's cow pasture. I can't tell you how many times I had to stop my car and wait for a herd of cows to cross the road. It got so bad that one of the local kids set up a "cow crossing guard" station and started charging people a dollar to clear the way. Smart kid—he probably made more money that summer than I did.

Cursing the GPS

Technology is supposed to make our lives easier, but if you've ever tried to use a GPS during road construction season in Wisconsin, you know that's a lie. The GPS lady confidently tells you to "turn right in 500 feet," but what she doesn't know is that there's a giant hole in the road and a crew of construction workers who definitely didn't get the memo about your travel plans.

One time, I was trying to get to a friend's house in Green Bay. My GPS gave me a nice, simple route—straight up Highway 41, with a couple of turns

at the end. Easy, right? Wrong. Halfway there, I hit a construction zone, and my GPS immediately went into panic mode. It started recalculating every five seconds, offering increasingly bizarre detour suggestions like "Turn left into the cornfield" and "Merge onto I-43, then drive directly into Lake Michigan."

By the time I reached my friend's house, I was ready to throw my GPS out the window. When I told my friend about my ordeal, he just laughed and said, "Next time, just follow the cows."

The Inexplicable Signs

One of the most confusing aspects of road construction in Wisconsin is the signage. You've got your basic "Road Closed" and "Detour" signs, but then there are the more cryptic ones, like "Lanes Shift Ahead" and "Bump." What does that mean? Which lanes? How much of a bump? Is this a metaphor for my life? The signs are like riddles, and the answers are never clear.

I once drove past a sign that said "End Construction" in the middle of a construction zone. It was like the workers just gave up halfway through and decided to call it a day. The road wasn't finished, the barrels were still up, and the pavement was uneven, but hey—according to the sign, construction was officially over.

Then there are the signs that contradict each other. You'll see a sign that says "Right Lane Closed," followed immediately by a sign that says "Left Lane Closed." So which lane am I supposed to use? I've tried honking at the signs to see if they'll answer, but so far, no luck.

The Rural Road Repairs

If you think the highways and main roads are bad, wait until you see the rural roads. In Wisconsin, rural road repairs are like a never-ending game of whack-a-mole. As soon as they fix one pothole, three more pop up in its place. And the repairs themselves are often questionable. I've seen potholes filled with everything from gravel to broken chunks of asphalt to what I'm pretty sure was leftover cheese curds.

One summer, the county decided to "resurface" the road that runs past my house. By "resurface," I mean they dumped a bunch of loose gravel on the road and called it a day. For the next three months, every time a car drove by, it sounded like a stampede of elephants. The gravel flew everywhere, denting mailboxes, shattering windows, and once, knocking over old man Jenkins' birdbath.

Jenkins wasn't too happy about that, so he marched down to the county office and demanded they fix the road. They did...by dumping more gravel on top of the old gravel. I guess they figured two layers of loose gravel are better than one. Jenkins eventually gave up and replaced his birdbath with a plastic one that he claims is "gravel-proof."

Why We Just Accept It

So why do we Wisconsinites put up with all this road construction nonsense? I think it's because we're used to making the best of things. We deal with freezing winters, mosquito-filled summers, and traffic jams caused by herds of cows. Road construction is just another challenge to overcome, and if there's one thing we're good at, it's overcoming challenges.

Plus, road construction season is a great excuse to swap stories and bond over shared experiences. Everyone's got a construction horror story, and sharing those stories is like a rite of passage. It's a way of saying, "Yeah, I've been there, too. We're all in this together."

I remember one summer when I was stuck in traffic for over an hour because the road crew decided to tear up both lanes of the highway at the same time. I finally reached the flagger at the front of the line, and I couldn't help but ask, "What's going on up there?"

The flagger shrugged and said, "I don't know, man. I just work here."

We both laughed, and for a moment, the frustration melted away. It was a small reminder that no matter how chaotic things get, there's always someone else going through it with you.

Embracing the Scenic Route

One of the silver linings of road construction season is that it forces you to take the scenic route. And if you're lucky, that scenic route might lead you to a hidden gem—a new supper club, a farm stand with fresh cheese curds, or a lake you never knew existed.

One summer, I got detoured through a little town called Luck. I'd never been there before, and I wasn't expecting much, but as I drove through the town, I stumbled upon a little diner called "The Lucky Spoon." I decided to stop in for lunch, and it turned out to be one of the best decisions I've ever made. The place had the best walleye sandwich I've ever tasted, and the waitress was so friendly that I felt like I'd known her my whole life.

If it hadn't been for that detour, I never would have discovered The Lucky Spoon. Now, every time I drive through Luck, I make a point to stop in and grab a walleye sandwich. And I have road construction to thank for that.

The Great Road Repair Debate

Of course, road construction season isn't just a hassle for drivers—it's also a hot topic of debate. Everyone's got an opinion on which roads need fixing, how long the repairs should take, and where the county is spending all that tax money. It's like an ongoing town hall meeting, except the only thing we can all agree on is that nothing ever gets done on time.

At the local diner, it's not uncommon to hear conversations like this:

"They've been working on Highway 12 for six months, and it's still not finished!"

"Six months? That's nothing. They've been fixing the same pothole on County Road P for three years!"

"Three years? I once saw a road crew fill a pothole with bubble gum and call it a day!"

It's all part of the great Wisconsin road repair debate—a never-ending cycle of complaints, conspiracies, and exaggerated stories that make you wonder if the road crew is secretly in cahoots with the local auto shops.

A Survival Guide for Road Construction Season

After decades of navigating Wisconsin's road construction season, I've come up with a few survival tips to help you keep your sanity intact:

❖ Plan for Detours: Always give yourself an extra 30 minutes to get anywhere, and be prepared to take a detour through a cornfield, a cow pasture, or possibly both.

❖ Embrace the Scenic Route: If you're going to get lost, you might as well enjoy the view. Look for hidden supper clubs, scenic lakes, and random roadside attractions like giant fiberglass fish statues.

❖ Stay Calm: When in doubt, take a deep breath, crack open a can of Leinenkugel's (not while driving, of course), and remember that this too shall pass—eventually.

❖ Make Friends with the Road Crew: If you see the same crew working on your road every day, take a moment to say hello. They're just as tired of the construction as you are, and they might have some insider info on when the road will actually be finished (spoiler alert: never).

❖ Keep a Sense of Humor: Road construction season is like winter in Wisconsin—it's long, it's inconvenient, and it's best endured with a little laughter and a lot of patience.

The End of Construction Season… Sort of

Eventually, road construction season comes to an end—or at least it slows down. The barrels get packed up, the detours are lifted, and for a brief, blissful moment, it feels like the roads are finally free. But deep down, we all know it's just a matter of time before the barrels come back, the signs go up, and we're once again navigating the chaos.

And you know what? That's okay. Because in Wisconsin, road construction is just another part of life. It's a reminder that nothing lasts forever—not the winter, not the roadblocks, and certainly not the gravel in old man Jenkins' driveway.

So the next time you find yourself stuck in traffic, waiting for a herd of cows to cross the road, or trying to decipher a cryptic detour sign, take a deep breath and remember: you're not alone. We've all been there, and we'll all be there again. And in the meantime, there's always The Lucky Spoon.

The Unwritten Rules of the Road in Wisconsin

For those driving through the Dairy State (and wanting to survive it)

1. **Wave at Everyone**
    If you pass another car on a country road, you're required by Wisconsin law (okay, not really, but close enough) to give a quick wave or at least the Midwestern *one-finger-off-the-steering-wheel salute*. If you don't, the other driver will assume you're from Illinois and gossip about it at the next fish fry.

2. **Slow Down for Deer, Speed Up for Potholes**
    If you see a deer on the side of the road, tap your brakes and proceed with extreme caution. However, if you encounter a pothole the size of Lake Winnebago, instinctually hit the gas to jump over it—your car's alignment and sanity depend on it.

3. **The Faster You Pass a Tractor, the Bigger the Wave**
    Passing a tractor on a two-lane highway? You've got to wave like you mean it—hand out, smile on, and maybe a "thanks, bud" head nod. Farmers own these roads, and you're just visiting.

4. **Four-Way Stops: It's Not About Who Got There First, It's About Who's Most Polite**
    In Wisconsin, a four-way stop is like a polite game of "Chicken." Nobody wants to go first. There will be so much waving and mouthing "No, you go!" that you'll all end up going at the same time and laughing about it at the Kwik Trip later.

5. **Always Stop for the Kwik Trip**
    If you see a Kwik Trip sign, it's mandatory to stop, even if you don't need gas. You always need something—a Glazer, a brat, or to say hi to your cousin Becky who works there. It's the Wisconsin equivalent of a pilgrimage.

6. **The "Drive-Thru U-Turn" Is Perfectly Acceptable**
If you miss your turn, don't bother making an illegal U-turn. Just drive through the nearest Culver's or Kwik Trip parking lot and loop around. Not only is this socially acceptable, but you can also grab a ButterBurger or a pack of cheese curds on the way.

7. **Speed Limits Are "Just a Suggestion" in the Country**
On a back road, the speed limit sign is more like a polite suggestion from the county—just don't tell Sheriff Bob I said that. The real rule? Drive fast enough to avoid getting stuck behind a tractor, but slow enough to enjoy the scenery and not hit a turkey.

8. **Salt Trucks Are Your Spirit Animal**
In winter, the sight of a salt truck is as welcome as a sunny day in January. If you see one, give a respectful nod, and maybe a heartfelt wave. They're the real MVPs of Wisconsin winters, and we all know it.

9. **The "First Snowfall" Is Practice for the Real Snow**
During the first snowfall of the season, everyone forgets how to drive. It's like we're all auditioning for a reality show called "Slip and Slide: Wisconsin Edition." The real rule is to leave extra space between you and the car in front—especially if their license plate says "ILLINOIS."

10. **If You Hear a Siren, Pull Over (and Start Gossiping)**
When an ambulance or fire truck goes by, you not only pull over, but you also start theorizing with your passenger about what could be happening. "Maybe it's old Mrs. Jensen again," or "I bet Carl's cow got loose again." Either way, it's going to be the talk of the post office.

11. **Don't Pass the Snow Plow—They Know Something You Don't**
Wisconsin snow plows are like the wise, experienced elders of the road. If you see one, stay behind it and follow at a respectful distance. Trust me, they're not slow for fun—they're slow because there's ice ahead waiting to ruin your day.

12. **Watch Out for Drunk Amish Buggies**
It's rare, but it happens. Late at night, those horse-drawn buggies can sometimes swerve a bit. Remember: it's not just the deer you have to watch for.

13. **The Left Lane on the Interstate Is Reserved for... No One**
Unlike other places where the left lane is the "fast lane," in Wisconsin, the left lane is more of a suggestion than a rule. Old man Jenkins driving 50 mph in a Buick will use it as he sees fit, and if you honk, he'll just glare at you in the mirror while turning up the polka music.

14. **Always Brake for Yard Sales, But Slam on the Brakes for a "Free" Sign**
Wisconsinites know the difference between "50% Off" and "Free"—and we know what matters. If you see a "Free" sign on a table of old fishing gear, slam on those brakes and be prepared to parallel park on the shoulder.

15. **Turn Signals Are Optional in December, Especially When Ice Fishing Gear Is Involved**
If you're hauling a trailer full of ice fishing gear, nobody expects you to use your turn signals. Your destination is obvious—to the nearest frozen lake—and everybody knows it.

16. **Culver's Curds Are Not Meant to Be Eaten in the Car, But We All Do It Anyway**

Everyone knows those cheese curds from Culver's are piping hot and come with a warning label, but if you wait until you get home to eat them, you're clearly not from here. Just burn your mouth quietly and don't let on to your passenger.

17. **A Green Bay Packers Sticker Means "I'm Not a Jerk," Unless You Cut Me Off**
If you see a Packers bumper sticker, it's an unspoken rule that this person is a decent human being. But if they cut you off, you'll probably let it slide... unless they have a Bears sticker too, in which case all bets are off.

18. **Tailgate Like You Mean It, Especially If There's a Roadside Brat Stand**
If you're stuck in traffic and spot a brat stand on the side of the road, feel free to pull off, grab a brat, and hop back in line. Everyone else in the traffic jam will understand, and someone might even ask you to grab them one too.

19. **Passing a "Fresh Cheese Curds" Sign is a Cardinal Sin**
If you see a sign that says "Fresh Cheese Curds," you're required by state tradition to stop. It doesn't matter if you're running late or if the car is full of groceries—just turn the wheel, say "Ope!" and grab those squeaky curds.

20. **If You're Not Sure Where You're Going, Just Follow the Guy with the Boat**
In Wisconsin, it's a safe bet that if you follow a truck with a boat hitched to it, you'll end up at a lake or a Kwik Trip. Either way, you're winning.

These unwritten rules of the road are what keep Wisconsin running (and us laughing). Whether you're navigating snowy back roads, cruising past cornfields, or merging onto the interstate at a brisk 62 mph, just remember: drive safe, be friendly, and don't ever forget to wave!

CHAPTER 6:
THE GREAT GREEN BAY MIGRATION

There are pilgrimages in this world that hold deep, spiritual meaning for people—journeys to sacred places that are life-changing. For Wisconsinites, our pilgrimage leads not to a temple or holy mountain, but to the frozen tundra of Lambeau Field, home of the Green Bay Packers. It's where we gather, not just to watch football, but to reaffirm our loyalty, our traditions, and our love for a team that's as much a part of Wisconsin as beer, brats, and snow.

Lambeau Field isn't just a stadium—it's the beating heart of Wisconsin. It's a place where strangers become friends, friends become family, and family becomes a screaming, cheese-wearing, face-painted mob. And twice a month during football season, the roads leading to Green Bay are filled with faithful fans making their way to the promised land. This is The Great Green Bay Migration.

The Journey Begins

If you've never been to a Packers game, let me paint a picture for you. It's a Sunday morning in late December. The temperature is hovering somewhere between "mild frostbite" and "hypothermia." Most people in their right mind would stay inside, wrapped in a blanket and sipping hot cocoa. But not in Wisconsin. No, in Wisconsin, we're piling into trucks and SUVs, dressed in 14 layers of clothing, ready to brave the elements and cheer on our beloved Packers.

For most fans, the journey to Lambeau begins at the crack of dawn. The parking lots open early—way earlier than seems reasonable—but that's all part of the experience. It's not just a football game; it's an all-day event. And if you don't get there early, you're not going to get a good spot to set up your grill.

I usually make the drive with my buddy Ed. Ed is the kind of guy who treats every Packers game like it's the Super Bowl. He's got a routine, a checklist, and a trunk full of supplies that would put a doomsday prepper to shame. Brats? Check. Cheese curds? Check. Enough beer to fill a kiddie pool? Double check.

We leave at dawn, coffee in hand, listening to pre-game analysis on the radio. The drive is mostly quiet—there's a sense of anticipation, like we're on a mission. Occasionally, we'll pass a car with Packers flags flying from the windows, and we'll exchange knowing nods. We're all part of the same migration, moving towards the same destination, united in our purpose.

The Tailgate Ritual

The true magic of a Packers game happens in the parking lot. Tailgating at Lambeau is an art form, perfected over generations. It's not just about grilling—it's about community, camaraderie, and the shared understanding that no amount of snow or wind can ruin a good bratwurst.

Ed takes his tailgating setup very seriously. He's got a portable grill, a folding table, and a cooler that could double as a life raft. He even has a special cheese slicer for his cheese curds, which he swears by. "It's all about presentation, Wayne," he says as he arranges the cheese curds in a neat circle on a paper plate.

Our fellow tailgaters are a mix of die-hard fans, seasoned veterans, and first-timers who have no idea what they're getting themselves into. There's always a group of college kids trying to outdo each other with creative face paint and homemade signs. And then there are the old-timers, dressed in full snowmobile gear, sipping brandy from thermoses like it's hot chocolate.

One of the best parts of tailgating at Lambeau is the food. You'll find everything from brats and burgers to venison chili and bacon-wrapped jalapeños. If it can be grilled, smoked, or deep-fried, someone's making it. I once saw a guy deep-frying cheese curds in the bed of his truck, using a portable fryer he'd rigged up with a propane tank. It was equal parts impressive and terrifying.

And of course, no tailgate is complete without a friendly debate about the Packers' chances that day. Everyone's got an opinion, and everyone thinks they're right. Old man Jenkins, who's been tailgating at Lambeau since the days of Bart Starr, likes to say, "The Packers could be 0-15, and I'd still believe they're going to the Super Bowl."

The Cheesehead Tradition

At some point during the tailgate, someone inevitably brings up the cheesehead hat. For those unfamiliar, the cheesehead is a large, foam wedge of cheese that Packers fans wear on their heads as a symbol of pride and loyalty. It started as a joke, but over the years, it's become a sacred tradition. To wear a cheesehead is to declare, "Yes, I am a proud Wisconsinite, and yes, I love cheese and football in equal measure."

My first cheesehead was a hand-me-down from my dad. It was a little worn around the edges, but it fit perfectly. I still wear it to every game, even though my wife insists that it's time for an upgrade. "That thing looks like it's been chewed on by a pack of dogs," she says, wrinkling her nose.

"Exactly," I reply. "It's got character."

Cheeseheads come in all shapes and sizes these days. Some fans customize their hats with Packers logos, lights, or even miniature beer cans. I once saw a guy with a cheesehead that doubled as a chip and dip tray. He was a hero that day.

Inside Lambeau Field

Walking into Lambeau Field for the first time is an experience I'll never forget. There's a certain reverence that comes with stepping onto the frozen tundra, like you're entering hallowed ground. The air is electric with anticipation, the stands are a sea of green and gold, and everywhere you look, there are fans cheering, singing, and waving their cheeseheads in the air.

For the uninitiated, the seating at Lambeau can be a bit of a shock. The seats are essentially long aluminum benches, with no individual chairs or armrests. It's a tight fit, especially when everyone's wearing four layers of clothing. But that's all part of the charm. You don't come to Lambeau for luxury—you come for the experience.

And what an experience it is. There's nothing quite like the roar of the crowd when the Packers score a touchdown, or the collective groan when the referees make a questionable call. It's like being part of one giant family, united in our joy, our frustration, and our undying love for the green and gold.

One of my favorite Lambeau traditions is the "Go Pack Go" chant. It starts with a small group of fans and spreads like wildfire, until the entire stadium is chanting in unison. It's a simple chant, but it never fails to give me chills. There's something powerful about being surrounded by thousands of people, all cheering for the same team, all believing in the same dream.

The Game Within the Game

While the action on the field is exciting, there's a whole other game happening in the stands. It's a game of strategic layering, as fans try to balance warmth with mobility. Too many layers, and you'll feel like the Michelin Man. Too few layers, and you'll freeze to the aluminum bench. It's a delicate dance, and everyone's got their own strategy.

My buddy Ed has a system that he swears by. He starts with a thermal base layer, followed by a fleece hoodie, a down jacket, and a waterproof parka. For his legs, he wears thermal leggings, jeans, and snow pants. And of course, he tops it all off with his lucky cheesehead.

"Layering is key, Wayne," he tells me as we shuffle into the stands. "You can always take off a layer, but you can't put one on if you didn't bring it."

Ed's system works, but it does have one major flaw: bathroom breaks. I once watched him try to navigate his way through a crowded row of fans, wearing what looked like 20 pounds of winter gear. It was like watching a penguin waddle through a minefield.

Packers Superstitions

If there's one thing Packers fans are known for, it's their superstitions. We're a superstitious bunch, and we'll do whatever it takes to ensure a victory. Some fans wear the same jersey to every game, others have lucky socks, and a few have rituals that are so elaborate, they could pass for ancient ceremonies.

I have a neighbor named Gary who takes his superstitions to the next level. He insists on sitting in the exact same spot on his couch for every game, wearing the same Packers hoodie he's had since 1996. If the Packers start losing, he'll switch to his backup lucky hat, which he claims has "special powers."

One game, the Packers were down by two touchdowns, and Gary was getting desperate. He turned to his wife and said, "Quick, get the emergency bratwurst!"

Apparently, the "emergency bratwurst" is a brat that Gary keeps in the freezer for situations like this. He believes that grilling the emergency brat during the fourth quarter will bring the Packers good luck. I'm not sure if it actually works, but I'll tell you this—the Packers won that game, and Gary's been grilling emergency brats ever since.

The Aftermath of a Packers Loss

As much as we love our Packers, we have to admit that they don't always win. And when they lose, it's like a dark cloud descends over the entire state. People walk around in a daze, heads hung low, silently questioning their life choices. It's like a collective mourning period, and the only thing that seems to help is beer and cheese curds.

After a particularly rough loss, Ed and I stopped at a bar on the way home from Lambeau. The place was packed with dejected fans, all staring into their drinks like they'd just witnessed the end of the world. The bartender, who looked like he'd seen this scene play out a thousand times, poured us each a drink and said, "Tough game, huh?"

"Yeah," I sighed, taking a sip of my beer. "Real tough."

But as the night went on, the mood started to lighten. People began sharing stories about past games, making jokes, and toasting to the hope of next season. By the time we left, the bar was filled with laughter and cheers. Because in Wisconsin, even in defeat, we find a way to come together and keep the faith.

The Drive Home

The drive home from a Packers game is always a bittersweet experience. If the Packers won, there's a sense of euphoria—a feeling that everything is right with the world. If they lost, there's a quiet resolve, a determination to come back stronger next time.

As Ed and I make our way home, we listen to post-game analysis on the radio, dissecting every play, every call, every decision. We talk about what went right, what went wrong, and what we hope to see next week. It's a ritual that never changes, no matter how many games we've been to.

By the time we pull into the driveway, we're already looking forward to the next game, the next tailgate, the next chance to gather with friends and family and cheer on our team. Because for us, the Packers aren't just a football team—they're a way of life.

A State United

In the end, the Great Green Bay Migration isn't just about football—it's about community. It's about coming together with people who share your passion, your traditions, and your love for a team that's been part of your life for as long as you can remember. It's about creating memories, forging friendships, and finding joy in the little things, like a perfectly grilled brat or a well-worn cheesehead.

So if you ever find yourself in Wisconsin on a Sunday morning, and you see a line of cars heading north towards Green Bay, don't be surprised. It's just the Great Green Bay Migration, and you're welcome to join us. Just remember to bring a brat, a beer, and a sense of adventure.

And if you happen to have a lucky cheesehead? Even better.

Lambeau Field Game Day Prep Checklist
For a True Wisconsin Tailgate Experience

Going to Lambeau Field is more than just attending a game—it's a **religious experience**. Whether you're a first-timer or a seasoned cheesehead, proper preparation is essential. So, grab your gear, load up your cooler, and don't forget your lucky socks. Here's your essential checklist for a successful pilgrimage to the Frozen Tundra.

1. Layer Up Like a Human Onion

☐ **Base Layer:** Long underwear, thermal socks, and anything that makes you feel like you're wearing a warm hug.

☐ **Middle Layer:** Packers hoodie or sweatshirt (preferably one you've been wearing since the '90s).

☐ **Top Layer:** Packers jacket, because you need to advertise your loyalty multiple times.

☐ **Emergency Layer:** That big, puffy coat you swore you'd never wear in public—yes, it's coming with you. It's Lambeau, not Milan.

☐ **Bonus Layer:** Extra pair of socks (because you'll lose feeling in your toes by halftime, and that's when the real fans double up).

2. Secure Your Lucky Game Day Attire

☐ **Jersey** (Rodgers, Favre, or any player from the last 20 years—if it's not stained with at least three types of dip, is it even lucky?)

☐ **Cheesehead Hat:** Make sure it's been properly aired out and doesn't smell like that one incident after the Vikings game.

☐ **Brat-Stained Packers Scarf:** Not only a fashion statement but also proof of your dedication. Bonus if it doubles as a napkin.

☐ **Thermal Gloves:** Yes, you'll have to take them off to drink beer, but think of them as a "heat reset button."

3. Tailgate Provisions

☐ **Brats (Obviously):** More than you think you'll need. Add five more. Now you're close.

☐ **Cheese Curds:** Fresh and squeaky—none of that rubbery nonsense.

☐ **Beer:** Lots of it. Preferably local and something hearty enough to withstand the Wisconsin cold.

- ☐ **Grill:** This is not the time to show up with an electric grill. Charcoal or propane, and don't forget the brat tongs.
- ☐ **Secret Family Recipe Dip:** You know the one—your uncle will disown you if you don't bring it.
- ☐ **Hot Cocoa Flask:** Partly for warmth, partly to sneak in something "special" to keep the cold away.

4. Tailgate Tools and Essentials

- ☐ **Folding Chairs:** Preferably the ones with built-in drink holders and 100% guaranteed to sink unevenly in the parking lot snow.
- ☐ **Portable Speaker:** Gotta blast that polka remix of the Packers fight song to let everyone know you're serious.
- ☐ **Cooler (The Big One):** Stocked with beverages and cheese curds to share with neighboring tailgaters (because we're all family here).
- ☐ **Green and Gold Face Paint:** Apply liberally; ignore friends who suggest subtlety.
- ☐ **Grilling Apron:** Bonus points if it says something like "Grillin' in a Blizzard" or "Kiss the Cook—After the Packers Win."

5. Lambeau Game Day Strategy

- ☐ **Pre-Game Rituals:** High-five strangers, chug a beer for luck, and lead a chorus of "Go Pack Go!" in the parking lot.
- ☐ **Plan for Weather Shifts:** Wisconsin weather can turn on a dime. Bring a poncho, hand warmers, and an extra blanket for the unexpected snowstorm during the fourth quarter.
- ☐ **Strategic Bathroom Line Assessment:** Identify the shortest lines before halftime, because you'll need to move quickly during the break—or prepare to do the *Lambeau Limbo* while waiting.
- ☐ **Chant Practice:** You need to be able to hit "Go Pack Go" with the intensity of a thousand brats sizzling on the grill. Save your voice for the "Kuuuuhn!" chant if you're old school.

6. Game Day Essentials Bag

- ☐ **Hand Warmers:** Trust me—bring extras. You'll end up giving them to a freezing stranger or your own feet.
- ☐ **Binoculars:** Not because you can't see the field, but because you need to keep an eye on the Bears fans three rows over.

☐ **Snacks for the Game:** Hidden pockets full of cheese sticks, beef jerky, and the obligatory small bag of cheese curds.

☐ **Portable Phone Charger:** You'll want enough battery to capture Lambeau Leaps, crowd waves, and your emotional breakdown when the Packers score in overtime.

7. Know Your Lingo

☐ **"Ope!"** You'll use it when someone bumps into you, when you drop a cheese curd, or when you forget where you parked.

☐ **"You betcha!"** The correct response to anyone asking if you're ready for game day.

☐ **"Da Bears Still Suck!"** Anytime someone brings up the rivalry, this phrase should be at the ready, especially if there are Chicago fans nearby.

☐ **"We Goin' to the Super Bowl!"** Say it early and often—before kickoff, at halftime, and especially after a few drinks.

8. Mental Prep for Lambeau Field

☐ **Prepare for Spontaneous Hugging:** High-fives, hugs, and impromptu victory dances are common after every Packers touchdown. If you're anti-hug, Lambeau might not be the place for you.

☐ **Brush Up on Your Tailgate Etiquette:** Share your cheese curds, compliment your neighbor's brat, and never, under any circumstances, root for the Vikings.

☐ **Study the Lambeau Leap Form:** You never know when you'll be called upon to explain or demonstrate the mechanics of the perfect Leap to an out-of-towner.

9. Post-Game Plan

☐ **Celebrate (or Console) with Custard:** Win or lose, Culver's custard is the answer.

☐ **Dissect the Game Over Beers:** Head to the nearest dive bar, order a round of Old Fashioneds, and passionately debate play calls as if Coach LaFleur is sitting at the next table, taking notes.

☐ **Secure Your Ride Home:** Whether it's a sober cousin, an Uber, or a snowmobile parked discreetly nearby, have a plan that doesn't end with you trying to sled your way home from the stadium.

10. Have Fun and Be Polite

- ☐ **Keep the Cheesehead High:** Whether it's a victory or a tough loss, keep your spirits up, be polite, and remember that every Packers fan is part of the family (yes, even Cousin Joe from Illinois).
- ☐ **Wave Goodbye Like a Pro:** As you leave the stadium parking lot, don't forget to wave at every single car, pedestrian, and dog. It's a long-standing tradition, and breaking it is practically sacrilege.

Now you're ready to tackle Lambeau Field like a true cheesehead. Follow this checklist, enjoy the camaraderie, and remember: at Lambeau, it's more than just a game—it's a **way of life**. Go Pack Go!

CHAPTER 7:
SURVIVING THE GREAT MOSQUITO WAR

If you ask someone who isn't from Wisconsin what they think the state's most dangerous creature is, they might say a bear or a wolf. Maybe they'd guess a rabid raccoon or an angry goose. But those of us who live here know better. We know that the true apex predator of the Midwest isn't a bear or a wolf—it's the mosquito. And if you think I'm exaggerating, you've clearly never tried to enjoy a Wisconsin summer without half a gallon of bug spray.

The Wisconsin mosquito is no ordinary mosquito. It's bigger, meaner, and hungrier than its counterparts in other states. It's a relentless blood-sucking menace, and it has a sixth sense for finding the one square inch of your skin that isn't covered in DEET. Surviving a Wisconsin summer is like fighting a war, and the mosquitoes are the enemy.

The Great Mosquito Awakening

The first warm evening of the year is a magical time in Wisconsin. The snow has finally melted, the air is filled with the scent of blooming flowers, and the sunsets last until well past 8 p.m. It's the kind of evening that makes you forget all about the frozen hellscape you just endured for five months. You think to yourself, "Maybe this is the year the mosquitoes won't be so bad."

But then, as you're sitting on the deck, enjoying a cold beer and listening to the crickets chirp, you hear it—a faint buzzing sound. You brush it off, telling yourself it's just one mosquito. But then you hear it again, and again, and before you know it, you're surrounded by a swarm of mosquitoes that look like they've been training for this moment all winter.

That's when you realize: the war has begun.

Mosquito Defense Strategies

Wisconsinites have developed a variety of defense strategies for surviving mosquito season. Over the years, I've seen everything from homemade bug sprays to elaborate citronella setups that look like something out of a tiki-themed wedding. Everyone's got their own method, and everyone swears by it.

My neighbor Gary, for example, believes that garlic is the key to repelling mosquitoes. He eats a raw clove of garlic every morning during mosquito season, claiming that it makes his blood "unappealing" to the little bloodsuckers. I don't know if that's true, but I do know that Gary smells like an Italian restaurant, and his wife refuses to sit next to him at cookouts.

My aunt Marge, on the other hand, is a firm believer in dryer sheets. She stuffs them into her pockets, tucks them into her hat, and even rubs them on her skin. "Mosquitoes hate the smell of dryer sheets," she insists. I'm not sure if that's scientifically accurate, but Marge's clothes are always wrinkle-free, so I guess there's that.

Then there's Ed, who swears by his homemade mosquito trap. It's a contraption made out of a plastic soda bottle, some sugar water, and a little bit of yeast. The idea is that the mosquitoes are attracted to the sugar water, fly into the bottle, and can't get out. Ed calls it his "mosquito death trap," and he's so proud of it that he shows it off to anyone who comes over.

"Look at that," he says, holding up the bottle and shaking it so we can see the mosquitoes inside. "That's two days' worth of mosquitoes. You're welcome."

The Mosquito Battle of Fourth of July

Every summer, my family hosts a big Fourth of July cookout at our cabin by the lake. It's a tradition that goes back generations, and it's always a good time—lots of food, lots of fireworks, and lots of beer. But it's also prime mosquito season, which means that every year, we find ourselves fighting the same battle against the mosquitoes.

One year, the mosquitoes were especially bad. The air was thick with humidity, and the lake was practically a breeding ground for the little devils.

My cousin Dave tried to set up one of those big bug zappers, but all it did was attract more mosquitoes. It sounded like a fireworks show in reverse—constant zaps followed by a faint, high-pitched sizzle.

After about an hour of swatting mosquitoes and slathering ourselves in bug spray, we decided to take drastic measures. My Uncle Larry—who, for the record, is the least outdoorsy person I know—suggested that we build a smoke screen. His idea was to set up a circle of citronella candles, tiki torches, and small bonfires around the perimeter of the yard, creating a barrier of smoke that would keep the mosquitoes at bay.

It was a bold plan, and I had my doubts, but desperate times call for desperate measures. So we lit the candles, fired up the torches, and started piling brush onto the bonfires. Within minutes, the yard was filled with thick, acrid smoke that made it hard to see, breathe, or enjoy the hot dogs.

But you know what? It worked. The mosquitoes stayed away, and we were finally able to relax—at least until the fire department showed up.

Apparently, one of our neighbors saw the smoke and called 911, thinking the cabin was on fire. When the firefighters arrived, we had to explain that no, we weren't burning down the cabin—we were just trying to keep the mosquitoes away. They didn't seem amused, but they let us off with a warning and a lecture about fire safety.

"Next time, try citronella spray," one of the firefighters suggested as he packed up the hose.

"Where's the fun in that?" Uncle Larry muttered.

Mosquitoes vs. Mosquito Spraying

In some places, the local government tries to control the mosquito population by spraying insecticide from trucks that drive through the neighborhoods at night. They call it "mosquito fogging," but I like to call it "chemical warfare." You're sitting in your living room, minding your own business, when suddenly you hear a low rumbling sound outside. You look out the window, and there it is—a white truck, slowly creeping down the street, spraying a thick cloud of mosquito-killing fog behind it.

For some reason, the truck always seems to drive by when you're outside grilling. One summer, Ed and I were in the middle of cooking up a batch of brats when we heard the truck coming. "Here comes the bug juice!" Ed yelled, waving his tongs like a madman.

We scrambled to cover the food, holding our breath as the truck passed by, leaving a trail of fog in its wake. After the fog cleared, we uncovered the grill and inspected the damage. The brats were fine, but the buns tasted faintly of chemicals. We decided to eat them anyway, figuring that a little extra pesticide wouldn't kill us.

The Mosquito Hunting Expedition

One summer, my buddy Carl came up with a wild idea: a mosquito hunting expedition. The idea was simple—gather a group of friends, arm ourselves with electric bug zappers, and spend an evening hunting mosquitoes around the lake. It sounded ridiculous, but Carl was so enthusiastic about it that we couldn't say no.

We all met at Carl's cabin, where he handed out electric bug zappers that looked like oversized tennis rackets. "These babies are top of the line," Carl said, grinning. "One swing, and those mosquitoes are toast."

We spent the next hour running around the yard, swinging our zappers like we were in a high-stakes game of mosquito tennis. Every time someone made contact, there was a satisfying zap followed by the smell of singed bug. It was strangely therapeutic.

By the end of the night, we were exhausted, covered in bug bites, and completely out of bug spray. But we felt victorious—like we'd fought the good fight and come out on top.

"Well," Carl said, wiping sweat from his forehead. "I think we made a dent in the population."

"Yeah," I replied, swatting one last mosquito off my arm. "We got, like, ten of them."

Carl nodded, looking proud. "That's ten fewer mosquitoes to ruin our summer."

Accepting the Mosquitoes

No matter how hard we try, the truth is that we're never going to win the war against the mosquitoes. They're too relentless, too numerous, and too good at finding new places to breed. But that doesn't mean we give up. It just means we learn to live with them—and maybe even find a little humor in the situation.

Over the years, I've come to accept that mosquito season is just part of life in Wisconsin. It's like winter—you know it's coming, you can't avoid it, and you just have to make the best of it. So you slather on the bug spray, light a few citronella candles, and try not to lose your mind when you hear that familiar buzzing in your ear.

And when all else fails, you can always crack open a cold beer, sit back, and watch the bug zapper do its thing.

A Lesson in Resilience

In the end, surviving mosquito season is a lesson in resilience. It's a reminder that life isn't always perfect, and sometimes you have to deal with a few blood-sucking pests to enjoy the good things—like warm summer nights, lakefront cookouts, and lazy afternoons spent fishing on the dock.

Sure, the mosquitoes are a pain in the neck (literally), but they're also a part of what makes Wisconsin, well, Wisconsin. They're a challenge to overcome, a shared enemy to unite against, and a source of endless stories and laughter.

So the next time you find yourself swatting mosquitoes on a warm summer night, remember this: you're not alone. We're all in this together, fighting the same battle, and doing our best to enjoy the fleeting warmth of a Wisconsin summer.

And if you ever find yourself at a Fourth of July cookout, surrounded by a circle of citronella candles, tiki torches, and small bonfires, just go with it. It may not be the most conventional way to keep the mosquitoes away, but it's a tradition—and in Wisconsin, tradition is everything.

The Official, Unofficial Guide to Wisconsin's Wildlife

Featuring the Real, the Mythical, and the Cheese-Loving

1. **The Wisconsin White-Tailed Deer**
   Our unofficial state mascot and the reason half the cars in Wisconsin have at least one cracked bumper. They're everywhere—fields, backyards, and especially the side of the highway at dusk. The deer's primary goal in life is to wait until you're going 60 mph, then cross the road in slow motion, giving you a look that says, *"Good luck, buddy."*

2. **The Cheesehead Badger**
   Wisconsin's official state animal and a creature as stubborn as a die-hard Packers fan in January. Badgers dig holes, give you a glare that says, *"You want a piece of this?"*, and refuse to admit defeat—even when faced with lawnmowers. Much like a typical Wisconsinite arguing about the best brat recipe.

3. **The Spotted Cow Sniffer**
   Legend has it that this mythical creature is drawn to the scent of New Glarus Spotted Cow beer. Sightings have been reported around backyard barbecues, tailgates, and fish fries. If you leave a cold bottle unattended, don't be surprised to see one trying to sip from it.

4. **The Great Midwestern Mosquito**
   The unofficial state bird of Wisconsin. Known for their ability to find any exposed skin within seconds and ruin any outdoor event. Rumor has it that the mosquitoes here are strong enough to carry off small pets, and they regard bug spray as just "seasoning."

5. **The Friendly Culver's Coyote**
   Coyotes in Wisconsin are known to be seen lurking near the outskirts of town and around Culver's dumpsters, likely plotting their next

move to sneak into the restaurant for a ButterBurger. They're surprisingly polite, only rummaging through the trash after hours and howling in what can only be described as a midwestern accent.

6. **The Crafty Raccoon (AKA The Northwoods Bandit)**
This raccoon doesn't just raid your garbage—it does it with style. It's got a knack for breaking into coolers at campsites, stealing brats off the grill, and giving you a *"What are you gonna do about it?"* look before waddling away. Local legend says raccoons know how to play Euchre if you give them a six-pack.

7. **The Kwik Trip Crow**
A true urban scavenger, known for frequenting the parking lots of Kwik Trips across the state. It's rumored that these crows are smarter than most high school students when it comes to navigating a drive-thru. They have a keen eye for dropped Glazers and discarded coffee cups.

8. **The Cornfield Turkey**
You'll find these hefty birds strutting around like they own the place. They appear out of nowhere, especially during hunting season when they develop invisibility powers. On other days, they're the Wisconsin equivalent of jaywalkers, taking their sweet time to cross the road, daring you to honk.

9. **The Great Lake Loon**
Known for its eerie call that sounds like a ghost haunting the lakes of the Northwoods. Loons are elegant swimmers and loyal to their territory, much like Packers fans with their parking spots. They also have a talent for photobombing sunset lake photos, looking majestic while you try to look relaxed.

10. **The Suburban Squirrel**
This feisty critter has a Ph.D. in bird feeder theft and is known for taking running leaps from the roof to your bird feeder, executing

stunts that would make Evil Knievel proud. If you catch one in the act, it'll freeze and pretend to be a statue, hoping you're as easily fooled as it thinks you are.

11. The Northern Pike (AKA "The Lake Shark")

Lurking in Wisconsin's lakes and rivers, the Northern Pike is known for its sharp teeth and tendency to scare unsuspecting kayakers and swimmers. Fishermen swear they've seen pike big enough to drag a canoe backwards, but it's possible they had a few too many Spotted Cows that day.

12. The Dairy Farm Cat

These tough, no-nonsense felines have been running Wisconsin farms for generations. They keep mice in line and act as unofficial supervisors in the barn, offering judgmental stares to any farmer not milking fast enough. Some claim these cats understand everything, but they refuse to share their secrets.

13. The State Fair Pig

Raised with the specific purpose of being the star attraction at the Wisconsin State Fair. Known for posing for photos, stealing fries off of kids' plates, and generally looking way too relaxed given the impending blue ribbon competition. They're also known to be the only animals that understand the appeal of deep-fried butter.

14. The Craft Brew Beaver

Not quite as industrious as its cousins up north, this beaver prefers hanging out near breweries, building dams just close enough to disrupt the water supply and give brewers something to complain about. It's rumored that beavers are trying to start their own microbrewery called *"Dam Good Beer."*

15. The Fishing Camp Crappie

This little fish is the pride and joy of every Wisconsin fishing camp. Kids love catching them because they're easy to reel in, and uncles love exaggerating their size by at least five inches. The crappie's main talent is convincing everyone it's better eating than it really is.

16. **The Brat-Loving Seagull**
    Commonly found at lakefronts and festival grounds, these seagulls have mastered the art of swooping in at the exact moment someone's distracted by their phone or chatting with their friend. Known for stealing hot dogs, brats, and the occasional cheese curd right out of the hand of unsuspecting tourists.

17. **The Snowplow-Watching Red-Tailed Hawk**
    This bird sits on fence posts along the highway, silently judging your driving skills in a snowstorm. It has an uncanny knack for appearing during whiteouts, making eye contact, and telepathically communicating, *"Maybe slow down a bit there, bud."*

18. **The Wisconsin Woolly Bear Caterpillar**
    The caterpillar that everyone swears can predict the harshness of winter. If it's got a lot of black on it, it means we're in for a long one. Wisconsinites have more faith in this fuzzy forecaster than they do in the local weatherman.

19. **The Tailgating Golden Retriever**
    You'll find this good boy at every tailgate, happily accepting brats, pats, and head scratches. He's wearing a little Packers jersey, wagging his tail in time with the fight song, and probably knows Lambeau better than half the fans. A true Wisconsinite at heart, he's a loyal friend, unless someone else has cheese.

20. **The Friday Night Fish Fry Catfish**
    This slippery critter is the one you hear stories about at every Wisconsin bar. "The biggest catfish I ever saw" is a staple tale, and no two stories are ever the same. This catfish is believed to be nearly a century old, have a hook collection in its mouth, and know all the fishing regulations better than the DNR.

Honorable Mention: The Wisconsin Sasquatch
Wisconsinites claim this elusive creature resides in the Northwoods, lured by the scent of grilling brats and the occasional bear keg. Some believe it's actually just Uncle Carl who got lost while trying to find his way back from deer camp, but sightings increase with every Packer loss and bottle of brandy.

Remember, these animals are as much a part of Wisconsin culture as the Packers, cheese curds, and frozen custard. So, keep an eye out on your next hike, camping trip, or Kwik Trip run—you never know what Wisconsin critter you might encounter!

Chapter 8:
Supper Clubs and Grasshopper Dreams

If there's one thing that's quintessentially Wisconsin, it's the supper club. And no, I'm not talking about those fancy city joints with dress codes and sommeliers who describe the wine in words longer than your arm. I'm talking about the classic, family-owned supper clubs you'll find scattered across Wisconsin, often tucked away on a country road or overlooking a lake. These places are like time capsules, preserving an era when "dining out" meant steak, shrimp, and enough brandy Old Fashioneds to fill a kiddie pool.

Wisconsin supper clubs are more than just restaurants—they're social institutions. They're where locals go to celebrate birthdays, anniversaries, Friday nights, and "made it through another week" triumphs. They're where you find the best prime rib, the coldest relish trays, and the most unapologetically boozy ice cream drinks. And the best part? It doesn't matter if you're a regular or a first-timer—everyone's treated like family.

The Anatomy of a Supper Club

To truly understand the Wisconsin supper club experience, you need to know a few key features. First and foremost is the relish tray. If you're not from here, you might be confused when a waitress plunks down a tray of pickled beets, carrot sticks, and cheese spread as soon as you sit down. The relish tray is a rite of passage, a Wisconsin appetizer that predates chips and salsa by decades. It's not just food—it's tradition.

Every supper club worth its salt also has a signature cocktail—usually a brandy Old Fashioned. Now, you can order an Old Fashioned in other parts of the country, but it won't be the same. In Wisconsin, we do things differently. Our Old Fashioneds are made with brandy, not bourbon, and they come loaded with fruit—orange slices, cherries, the works. And we like them sweet, which is why you'll often see folks ordering them with 7-Up instead of soda water. Purists may scoff, but we don't care. It's our drink, and we're proud of it.

Then there's the fish fry. I know I've already talked about Friday night fish fry, but supper clubs take it to another level. They serve up crispy, golden-brown fish with sides of coleslaw, potato pancakes, and rye bread. And if you ask nicely, they'll throw in a lemon wedge and a side of homemade tartar sauce. It's not just a meal—it's a work of art.

Finally, no supper club experience is complete without a grasshopper—the minty ice cream drink that's practically dessert and a cocktail all rolled into one. A grasshopper is a delicate balance of crème de menthe, crème de cacao, and vanilla ice cream, blended together until it's smooth and frothy. It's like drinking a boozy shamrock shake, and it's the perfect way to end a meal.

My First Supper Club Experience

I still remember my first trip to a supper club. I was eight years old, and my parents decided to take me and my sister to The Pine Tree Lodge, a classic supper club just outside of town. I was too young to appreciate the history or the ambiance, but I remember being fascinated by the big neon sign out front—a giant pine tree with flashing green lights that seemed to beckon us inside.

When we walked in, I was hit with the smell of prime rib and cigarette smoke (back in those days, people smoked everywhere). The place was packed, and the bar was lined with people sipping Old Fashioneds and laughing like old friends. I remember thinking it felt like a big family gathering, even though I didn't know most of the people there.

My parents ordered the prime rib, and my sister got the shrimp cocktail, but all I wanted was the relish tray. I'd never seen one before, and I was intrigued by the assortment of pickles, olives, and little white crackers that looked like they belonged in a dollhouse. I picked up a cracker, spread some cheese on it, and popped it in my mouth. It was like eating heaven on a Ritz.

When dessert time rolled around, my dad ordered a grasshopper for the table. I had no idea what it was, but when it arrived, I was mesmerized. It was bright green, topped with whipped cream and a cherry, and it looked like something out of a cartoon. My dad let me have a sip, and I was hooked. From that moment on, I knew that supper clubs were my kind of place.

The Supper Club Debate

Now, like any self-respecting Wisconsinite, I've got strong opinions about supper clubs. My buddy Jim and I have had more than a few heated debates about which supper club is the best. Jim swears by Al's Lakeview, while I'm a loyal fan of The Pine Tree Lodge. Our debates usually go something like this:

Jim: "Al's Lakeview has the best fish fry in the state."

Me: "No way. The Pine Tree Lodge's fish fry is crispy on the outside and flaky on the inside. It's perfection."

Jim: "Yeah, but Al's has potato pancakes that are so good, you'll want to write them a thank-you note."

Me: "Please. The Pine Tree Lodge's potato pancakes are a revelation. They've got just the right amount of crispiness, and they're not too greasy."

Jim: "But the Old Fashioneds at Al's are legendary."

Me: "The Pine Tree Lodge's Old Fashioneds could bring a tear to your eye. They're that good."

This back-and-forth goes on for hours, with no clear winner. In the end, we usually agree to disagree and plan our next supper club visit. After all, the only thing better than a good supper club meal is another good supper club meal.

The Supper Club Etiquette

There's a certain etiquette to dining at a supper club that every Wisconsinite knows instinctively. For starters, you should always arrive early and have a drink at the bar while you wait for your table. It's not just about passing the time—it's about soaking in the atmosphere and catching up with the locals. You might meet someone who knows your cousin, your neighbor, or your plumber's brother-in-law. And in Wisconsin, that counts as a close friend.

When you're at the bar, it's customary to order an Old Fashioned. You can ask for a beer, but you'll get a few raised eyebrows. And if you order a martini, the bartender will probably suggest you try the steak instead.

Once you're seated, you're expected to order an entrée that involves some kind of red meat or seafood. Chicken is acceptable, but only if it's smothered in gravy or stuffed with something delicious. And don't forget to order the potato pancakes—they're a must.

When dessert rolls around, you should always opt for the grasshopper, even if you're too full to move. It's a point of pride, like finishing a marathon or successfully parallel parking on the first try.

Supper Club Lore

Every supper club has its own lore—stories passed down from one generation of diners to the next. Some stories are about the owners, who've been running the place for decades. Others are about regulars who've been coming every Friday night since Eisenhower was in office. And some are about the meals themselves—like the legendary Steak Oscar at The Pine Tree Lodge, which supposedly saved a man's marriage (the details are fuzzy, but it definitely involved a lot of butter).

One of my favorite supper club legends is the story of "The Great Prime Rib Shortage of 1987." According to local lore, a particularly harsh winter storm caused a supply chain disruption, leaving The Pine Tree Lodge without its signature prime rib for an entire weekend. The regulars were devastated, and the waitstaff had to break the news gently, like telling a child their dog ran away. People ordered fish instead, but the mood was somber, and the night ended early.

The next weekend, when the prime rib finally returned, the place was packed. People came from miles around to celebrate, and the owners even put up a sign that read, "The Prime Rib is Back—Praise the Lord!" It's been a running joke ever since, and every year, they throw a little "Prime Rib Revival" to commemorate the event.

Why Supper Clubs Matter

There's something special about a Wisconsin supper club. It's not just the food, the drinks, or the ambiance—it's the sense of belonging. When you walk into a supper club, you're not just a customer—you're part of a tradition. You're stepping into a place where time seems to stand still, where the waitstaff knows your name, and where the bartender remembers your drink.

Supper clubs are a reminder of simpler times, when a night out meant good food, good company, and a good Old Fashioned. They're places where families gather to celebrate life's milestones, where friends catch up over a plate of fried fish, and where strangers become friends.

A Supper Club Dream

One night, after a particularly satisfying supper club meal, I had a dream. I was standing in the middle of a giant supper club, surrounded by relish trays, Old Fashioneds, and plates of prime rib. The walls were lined with family photos, and the bar was stocked with every brand of brandy known to man. There was a big neon sign that read, "Welcome Home, Wayne."

I wandered through the dining room, shaking hands with regulars, sampling potato pancakes, and chatting with the waitstaff like old friends. Everyone was smiling, and the air was filled with laughter and the clink of cocktail glasses. It felt like heaven—or at least a very well-decorated version of it.

When I woke up, I couldn't help but smile. It was just a dream, but it felt real—a reminder of all the supper clubs I've visited over the years, all the meals I've shared with friends and family, and all the memories I've made along the way.

A Place Called Home

In the end, supper clubs aren't just places to eat—they're places to belong. They're places where you can sit down, relax, and enjoy a meal with the people you care about. They're places where the food is hearty, the drinks are strong, and the atmosphere is warm and welcoming. And in a world that's always changing, that kind of place is something special.

So the next time you find yourself driving down a country road, and you see a neon sign flashing in the distance, don't pass it by. Pull over, grab a seat at the bar, and order an Old Fashioned. You might just discover a new favorite supper club—and a new tradition to call your own.

And if you happen to end the night with a grasshopper? Even better.

Classic Wisconsin Grasshopper Cocktail Recipe
With a Twist of Dairy State Humor

In Wisconsin, the Grasshopper isn't just a cocktail—it's a rite of passage and practically a dessert in a glass. This sweet, minty, creamy delight is perfect for cooling down after a fish fry, surviving the summer heat, or just showing your out-of-town guests how we do things *the right way*. So grab your ice cream scoop, put on your best supper club voice, and let's whip up a Grasshopper that'll make even Aunt Marge nod in approval.

Ingredients:

- **1 cup vanilla ice cream** (the kind that's so thick you have to wrestle it out of the tub)
- **1 oz crème de menthe** (the green stuff that makes it look like you're about to commit to a minty adventure)
- **1 oz crème de cacao** (because every good Wisconsinite knows that a little chocolate never hurt anyone)
- **1/2 cup whole milk** (none of that skim nonsense—it's called a "dessert drink" for a reason)
- **Whipped cream** (store-bought, homemade, or the kind you spray directly into your mouth—no judgment)
- **Chocolate shavings or sprinkles** (for when you're feeling fancy, or want to impress the in-laws)
- **Crushed graham crackers** (optional, but recommended for anyone who likes to overachieve)

Directions:

Step 1: Get Your Ice Cream Ready

- Dig out a cup of vanilla ice cream from that tub in the freezer. It's best if the ice cream is just slightly soft, but if you're working with rock-solid Wisconsin-grade dairy, don't worry—just tell it, *"Ope, sorry 'bout that,"* and let it sit for a minute. If it's melting too fast, you can apologize profusely to your ice cream like a true Midwesterner.

Step 2: Blend 'Er Up

- In a blender, add your **crème de menthe, crème de cacao,** and **whole milk.** Don't skimp on the booze, or your grandma will haunt you with disappointed glances.

- Toss in your **vanilla ice cream** and blend until smooth. If it's too thick to blend, just give the blender a gentle *"You can do it, buddy"* pep talk.
- Blend until the mixture is creamy and smooth, or until your blender sounds like it's trying to swallow a brick.

Step 3: Check the Consistency

- Pour a little into a glass to test the consistency. If it's thicker than the accent on an Eau Claire news anchor, you're doing it right. If it's too thin, add more ice cream until it reaches that *"So-thick-you'll-need-a-spoon-but-you'll-use-a-straw-anyway"* consistency.

Step 4: Pour and Top It Off

- Pour your Grasshopper into a chilled glass (or a plastic Packers cup if you're staying true to the Wisconsin aesthetic).
- Top generously with **whipped cream**—the kind that's so fluffy you could mistake it for a snowbank in January.
- If you're feeling classy, add some **chocolate shavings or sprinkles** on top. If you're not, go ahead and stick a cheese curd on the rim for decoration (hey, we don't judge creativity around here).
- Optional: sprinkle some **crushed graham crackers** on top. This is just in case you want to tell people you made a "gourmet cocktail."

Step 5: Serve with Pride

- Present your Grasshopper with confidence, knowing that you've made something special. If anyone questions your dessert-drink-making skills, just shrug and say, **"Well, this is how my grandma used to make it, so..."**
- Hand a glass to your guest and watch as their face lights up with nostalgia and brain-freeze.

Pro Tips for Grasshopper Greatness:

- **Double the Recipe** if you're making one for your neighbor, your spouse, and your third cousin who always shows up unannounced around dessert time.
- **Add More Booze** if the Packers are losing. This is an unspoken Wisconsin rule.
- **Always Keep Extra Ice Cream on Hand** in case your first glass "didn't turn out right" (translation: you drank it before anyone

noticed).

- If you're trying to *"lighten it up a bit,"* then what are you doing in Wisconsin?

Disclaimer:

If you drink too many of these, you may start speaking fluent "Midwest Nice," accidentally over-apologize to strangers, or enthusiastically offer to shovel your neighbor's driveway… in July. Drink responsibly!

Enjoy Your Classic Wisconsin Grasshopper!

Remember, the Grasshopper isn't just a cocktail—it's a state of mind. A creamy, minty, slightly boozy state of mind that pairs perfectly with cheese curds and a winning Packers game. Cheers! Or, as we say in Wisconsin, **"You betcha!"**

CHAPTER 9:
WINTER IS COMING (AND IT'S ALREADY HERE)

When people think of Wisconsin, the first thing that usually comes to mind is cheese. The second thing is beer. But right after that comes winter—the long, relentless, bone-chilling season that defines life in the Great White North. Around here, we don't just get a little snow or the occasional cold snap. No, we get full-blown winters that make Game of Thrones look like a spring break special.

We Wisconsinites like to joke that winter lasts eight months, and the other four months are just pre-winter. By the time October rolls around, we're already bracing for that first snowfall. The weather forecasters start using phrases like "polar vortex" and "Arctic blast," and the grocery stores fill up with people panic-buying bread and milk like the apocalypse is coming. And in a way, it is.

But if you ask a Wisconsinite how they feel about winter, they'll probably shrug and say, "Eh, it's not so bad." That's because we've been through it all before. We know how to survive, and we know how to make the best of it. After all, winter may be harsh, but it's also part of what makes Wisconsin special.

The First Snow

The first snowfall of the season is always a magical time. There's a hush in the air, a sense of anticipation, and the feeling that maybe, just maybe, this winter won't be so bad. The snowflakes start falling, covering everything in a soft, white blanket. Kids run outside to build snowmen, and parents stand at the window, sipping coffee and admiring the peaceful scene.

But that sense of wonder lasts for about 30 seconds, until you remember that you still have to shovel the driveway, scrape the ice off your car, and hope the snowplow doesn't bury your mailbox again. The magic wears off quickly, and you're left with the cold, hard reality of winter.

I remember one year, the first snowfall happened in early November. It wasn't much—just a light dusting—but people acted like it was the blizzard of the century. My neighbor Gary, who's a bit of an alarmist, was out there with his snowblower at the crack of dawn, clearing the driveway like he was preparing for a military invasion.

"Gary, it's just a dusting," I called out, trying not to laugh.

"Can't be too careful, Wayne," he replied, shaking his head. "You never know when it'll hit."

Sure enough, the next day, we got hit with a real snowstorm—nearly a foot of snow in one night. Gary looked like a prophet, and the rest of us were left scrambling to clear our driveways. The lesson? Never underestimate a Wisconsin winter.

The Art of Layering

Surviving winter in Wisconsin requires more than just a warm coat. It requires a strategic approach to layering that takes years to master. We're not talking about throwing on a sweater and calling it a day. We're talking about a complex system of thermal layers, moisture-wicking fabrics, and waterproof outerwear that could rival a NASA spacesuit.

For example, my winter routine starts with a base layer of thermal long johns, followed by a fleece-lined hoodie, a heavy-duty parka, and a pair of snow pants. I top it all off with a hat, scarf, and a pair of mittens so thick that I could probably catch a football made of ice.

My wife, on the other hand, takes a more minimalist approach. She wears a light jacket and a pair of gloves, and she seems perfectly content—even when the wind chill is well below zero. I don't know how she does it. I've asked her about her secret, and all she says is, "Mind over matter, Wayne." I think she's just too stubborn to admit she's cold.

Layering isn't just about staying warm—it's about being prepared. You never know when you'll need to shed a layer to avoid overheating in a crowded grocery store, or when you'll need to add an extra layer because the wind has decided to cut through your jacket like a hot knife through butter. It's a delicate balance, and only true Wisconsinites can pull it off with style.

Ice Fishing: A Freezing Good Time

If there's one winter activity that separates the true Wisconsinites from the pretenders, it's ice fishing. Now, I know what you're thinking: who in their right mind would willingly sit on a frozen lake in the middle of winter, staring at a hole in the ice? The answer: Wisconsinites. And we love it.

Ice fishing isn't just a sport—it's a way of life. It's a chance to escape the house, breathe in the crisp winter air, and bond with your buddies over the shared experience of freezing your tail off. It's also an excuse to drink beer and eat venison jerky, which is really the main reason we do it.

Every year, my buddy Carl organizes an ice fishing trip out on Lake Winnebago. He's got all the gear—an ice auger, a portable shanty, and enough bait to feed an army of fish. I tag along, mostly for the camaraderie and the chance to hear Carl's tall tales about the "monster walleye" he once caught. (For the record, I've never seen this monster walleye, but Carl swears it exists.)

The thing about ice fishing is that it's not really about catching fish. It's about the ritual—the setting up of the shanty, the drilling of the holes, and the quiet moments of reflection as you sit on a folding chair, sipping a cold beer and contemplating the mysteries of life. And if you do happen to catch a fish? That's just a bonus.

Surviving the Holidays

The holidays are a special time in Wisconsin, filled with family gatherings, festive decorations, and an endless supply of holiday treats. But they're also a time of stress, chaos, and the occasional bout of cabin fever. When you're cooped up in a house with extended family members for days on end, tensions can run high.

One Christmas, my family decided to spend the holidays at our cabin up north. It seemed like a great idea—snowy landscapes, cozy fires, and plenty of room for everyone. But by the third day, the cabin fever had set in. My Uncle Larry was complaining about the lack of cell service, my cousin Dave was hogging the TV to watch college football, and my aunt Marge was trying to feed us all leftover lutefisk from last year's Christmas dinner.

In an effort to break the tension, my dad suggested we go for a "refreshing walk" outside. This was Wisconsin code for "get out of the house before we all lose our minds." So we bundled up, put on our snowshoes, and trudged through the snow in silence, each of us quietly reflecting on our life choices.

The walk worked, though. By the time we got back to the cabin, everyone was in a better mood, and we managed to make it through the rest of the holiday without any major blowouts. And when it was all over, we raised a glass of eggnog and toasted to surviving another family Christmas.

The Snowplow Wars

If you live in Wisconsin, you know that snowplows are both a blessing and a curse. On one hand, they clear the roads and make it possible to leave your house. On the other hand, they have an uncanny ability to bury your driveway just as soon as you've finished shoveling it.

Every winter, I find myself locked in a battle of wits with the snowplow driver. I'll shovel my driveway, carefully clearing away the snow and creating a neat little path to the street. I'll stand there, admiring my handiwork, feeling a sense of pride and accomplishment. And then, without fail, the snowplow will come rumbling down the street and dump a fresh load of snow right at the end of my driveway.

"Are you kidding me?" I'll mutter, shaking my fist at the retreating snowplow.

But there's no point in getting mad. It's just part of the game. You shovel, the snowplow dumps, and the cycle continues until spring. It's like a dance—one that leaves you with sore arms and an aching back.

Embracing the Cold

At some point, every Wisconsinite has to come to terms with the cold. You can complain about it, you can try to avoid it, but eventually, you just have to embrace it. And once you do, you start to see winter in a different light.

For example, there's something oddly beautiful about the way the snow sparkles in the moonlight, or the way the ice on the lake cracks and groans like it's alive. There's a sense of quiet and stillness that you don't get in the warmer months—a kind of frozen tranquility that makes you appreciate the simple things.

And then there are the little joys of winter, like the first sip of hot cocoa after shoveling the driveway, or the feeling of taking off your boots and warming your toes by the fire. It's the kind of satisfaction that comes from enduring something difficult and coming out stronger on the other side.

A Love-Hate Relationship

In the end, winter in Wisconsin is a love-hate relationship. We love the cozy nights by the fire, the snow-covered landscapes, and the excuse to eat comfort food and drink hot toddies. But we hate the frozen pipes, the icy roads, and the constant battle with the snowplow.

It's a complicated relationship, but it's one that defines us as Wisconsinites. We don't just survive winter—we embrace it, with all its challenges and all its beauty. And when spring finally arrives, and the snow starts to melt, we breathe a sigh of relief and celebrate the fact that we made it through another winter.

But deep down, we know that winter will be back before we know it. And when it does, we'll be ready.

Blizzard Survival Tips: The Wisconsin Way

Because a little snow never hurt anyone (except Carl when he tried to shovel the roof).

1. **Stock Up on Bread, Milk, and Cheese Curds**
   During a blizzard, bread and milk fly off the shelves like they're the last tickets to a Packers game. But let's be honest—you really need **cheese curds** and **beer** to get through it. So load up on the essentials and maybe throw in a frozen pizza or six.

2. **Layer Up Until You're Practically Bulletproof**
   Wisconsin's motto during a blizzard: *"When in doubt, add another layer."* You should be wearing so many coats, scarves, and socks that you can't put your arms down or hear properly. The goal is to look like Ralphie's little brother from *A Christmas Story*, but with more Packers gear.

3. **Declare War on Your Driveway**
   When it starts snowing, your driveway becomes the enemy. Arm yourself with a shovel, a snowblower, or Carl's old flamethrower (if the HOA isn't looking). Shovel early, shovel often, and remember: the moment you finish, the snowplow will come by and bury it all again. Just accept it. It's Wisconsin karma.

4. **Keep the Good Sleds Inside**
   Every family has the *"good sleds"*—those sturdy plastic or metal beauties that have seen more action than a deer camp poker game. Keep them safe inside until you're ready to use them, or you'll find them buried under five feet of snow with the garden gnome by the time the blizzard ends.

5. **Create a Blizzard Drinking Game**
   For every inch of snow, take a sip of your favorite Wisconsin beverage. If the snowplow blocks your driveway again, that's a shot. Every time your neighbor tries to *"help"* by giving unsolicited advice

on your shoveling technique, that's two shots. You'll either get through this with a smile or pass out until it's all over.

6. **Find a Craft Project for When the Power Goes Out**
Whether it's knitting, whittling a new cheese spreader, or reorganizing your collection of Packers jerseys by year and level of nostalgia, you need something to do. If you've got kids, get ready for the classic *"Guess How Long We'll Be Stuck Inside"* game. Winner gets to pick the last frozen pizza.

7. **Check on the Neighbors... and By "Check," We Mean "Gossip"**
In Wisconsin, checking on your neighbors during a blizzard is a time-honored tradition. Make sure old Mrs. Jensen has enough firewood and then spend the next half hour gossiping about why Carl hasn't plowed his driveway yet and if Dave's new snowblower is really worth what he paid.

8. **Pretend You're Brave Enough to Grill Outside**
It's a Wisconsin tradition to talk about grilling in a blizzard like it's no big deal. But if you actually decide to do it, be prepared for your family to watch you through the window, laughing and taking pictures as you try to flip brats in 40 mph winds and sideways snow. Just smile and wave, and insist *"It's just like summer!"*

9. **Turn Snow Removal into a Neighborhood Competition**
You don't just shovel your driveway—you compete. If you see Carl's driveway looking clearer than yours, it's time to step up your game. Who can clear the sidewalk faster? Who has the straightest snow lines? If you win, you get bragging rights at the next fish fry.

10. **Bake a Hotdish Just to Warm the House**
Nothing warms the house and your soul like a big ol' hotdish. Toss in everything you've got—leftover ham, potatoes, three kinds of cheese, and a can of soup you didn't know you had. Stick it in the oven and

let the comforting aroma take your mind off the fact that you haven't seen your mailbox in two days.

11. Be Ready to Hear "Snowmageddon" on the News

When the TV meteorologist says, *"We've got a real Snowmageddon coming,"* you have to take a shot (of brandy, of course). If they say it twice in one segment, put on your favorite Packers onesie because you're not leaving the house until April.

12. Make the Ultimate Fort

If you've got kids—or if you're just a grown-up kid—it's time to build the ultimate snow fort. Carve out a small space in the snowdrifts, add a flag, and declare it a "snow-plow-free zone." And if the plow does come by and destroys it, make a new one and label it *"Fort Rebuilt to Spite the County."*

13. Use Your Snowblower Like You're Training for the Olympics

Nothing makes you feel more powerful than firing up the snowblower and making snow fly 20 feet in the air. Make sure to wear your best "I'm-doing-this-for-the-glory" face while operating it. And don't forget to aim the snow at the same spot the plow keeps dumping onto your driveway—it's a game of snowy revenge.

14. Embrace Cabin Fever with a Packer Themed Puzzle

You're going to be stuck inside, so you might as well embrace it. Break out that 1000-piece *"Lambeau Field in a Blizzard"* jigsaw puzzle and get ready for a journey that will test your patience, eyesight, and ability to avoid yelling at family members over who took the corner piece.

15. Throw Boiling Water in the Air (But Safely!)

If it's ridiculously cold, grab a cup of boiling water, head outside, and toss it into the air. Watch as it instantly turns to snow vapor and congratulate yourself on *"performing a scientific experiment."* Just be sure not to throw it directly into the wind, or you'll learn the hard way why

Carl's eyebrows are missing.

16. Play the "Find My Car" Game
If your car is buried in a snowdrift, it's time to play *"Find My Car."* The rules are simple: dig where you think you left it and hope for the best. If you find your neighbor's car instead, just move it to a random spot and see how long it takes them to notice.

17. Rescue the Gnomes
It's your duty to save the garden gnomes before they're buried until spring. Bonus points if you dress them in little scarves and Packers beanies. Your neighbors will think you're crazy, but in Wisconsin, we call that *"creative winter landscaping."*

18. Leave the Christmas Lights Up
Who are we kidding? You're not going to climb on a ladder in a blizzard to take down those lights. Just declare them *"winter lights"* and pretend it's intentional. By April, they'll be part of the family.

19. Prepare for Blistering Complaints About the Cold
Brace yourself for every conversation to start with, *"Can you believe this cold?"* followed by an obligatory 10-minute rant about how it *"wasn't this bad back in '78."* Smile, nod, and feel free to exaggerate your own "surviving the cold" stories. Everyone does.

20. Don't Let It Ruin Your Day
Blizzards are just part of life in Wisconsin. Embrace it, make the most of it, and remember that spring is (eventually) coming. In the meantime, hunker down, have another Grasshopper, and wait for the Packers highlights to come on TV. You've got this—*you betcha!*

CHAPTER 10:
THE HUNTING SEASON HUSTLE

In Wisconsin, there's a time of year that rivals the intensity of Packers season, the reverence of Friday night fish fries, and the excitement of a state fair cream puff eating contest. I'm talking about hunting season—the unofficial holiday that sweeps through the state every November, turning normally mild-mannered folks into a veritable army of orange-clad adventurers. Deer hunting isn't just a hobby in Wisconsin; it's a rite of passage, a cultural tradition, and a legitimate reason to take time off work and school.

When hunting season arrives, small towns turn into ghost towns, radio stations play more hunting updates than country hits, and local diners serve up extra-large plates of eggs and bacon to bleary-eyed hunters on their way to the woods. It's a spectacle like no other, and it's something that every true Wisconsinite holds dear to their heart.

The Orange Army

The first day of hunting season is like Christmas morning for hunters. Grown men and women wake up before dawn, dressed in layers of camo and blaze orange, armed with thermoses of coffee and enough snacks to last them through a snowstorm. They pack up their trucks, check their gear for the hundredth time, and hit the road in search of their deer stands.

It's a scene that plays out across the state, from the rolling hills of the Driftless Area to the deep forests of the Northwoods. And while every hunting camp is different, there are a few things they all have in common: a trusty old truck, a cooler full of venison sticks, and a radio tuned to the local station for the "Deer Report."

The Deer Report is a Wisconsin institution. It's a radio segment that provides updates on the weather, deer movement, and any notable bucks spotted in the area. Listening to the Deer Report is a sacred ritual, akin to reciting the pre-game lineup for the Packers. And while most of the information is just speculation, rumors, and tall tales, hunters take it very seriously.

One year, my buddy Jim called me at 5:30 a.m. to tell me he'd heard on the Deer Report that a "big ten-pointer" had been spotted near his hunting land. He was so excited, you'd think he'd just won the lottery. I didn't have the heart to tell him that the same big ten-pointer had been spotted in three different counties.

Camp Traditions and Tall Tales

If there's one thing hunters love more than hunting, it's telling hunting stories. And like all good stories, the details tend to get embellished over time. What starts as a modest eight-pointer can quickly become a twelve-pointer with antlers the size of bicycle handlebars.

At my family's hunting camp, we have a long-standing tradition of gathering around the campfire after a day in the woods to swap stories and share a drink or two. There's my Uncle Larry, who's always got a new story about the "one that got away," and my cousin Dave, who swears he once saw a deer wearing a reflective vest. (It turned out to be a hiker, but Dave refuses to acknowledge that.)

One of my favorite hunting stories comes from old man Jenkins, who claims he once bagged a buck with a broken ankle and a pocket knife. According to Jenkins, he was climbing into his tree stand when the ladder broke, sending him crashing to the ground and twisting his ankle in the process. As he lay there, nursing his injury, a buck walked right up to him. With no other options, Jenkins pulled out his pocket knife and…well, you can guess the rest.

"Did it really happen?" people ask.

"Doesn't matter," Jenkins replies with a wink. "Makes for a good story, don't it?"

The One That Got Away

Every hunter has a story about "the one that got away." It's a tale of near misses, misfires, and missed opportunities that haunts you long after the season ends. For me, it happened a few years back during the last day of rifle season.

I was sitting in my deer stand, half-asleep and half-frozen, when I heard a rustling in the bushes. My heart started racing, and I slowly turned my head to see a massive buck—easily a twelve-pointer—walking towards me. It was like something out of a hunting magazine. I held my breath, raised my rifle, and took aim.

But just as I was about to squeeze the trigger, the wind shifted, and the buck caught my scent. He bolted into the woods, leaving me sitting there with my rifle in hand and a dumbfounded look on my face.

I spent the rest of the day replaying the moment in my head, wondering what I could have done differently. When I got back to camp, I told the guys what had happened, expecting sympathy and understanding. Instead, they just laughed and slapped me on the back.

"Don't worry, Wayne," Jim said. "You'll get him next year. Or at least that's what you'll tell people."

Hunting Season Meals

While hunting season is technically about hunting, it's also about food. Specifically, the kind of hearty, stick-to-your-ribs meals that fuel you through a long day in the woods. Every hunting camp has its go-to meals, and in my family, that means venison stew, chili, and a breakfast dish we call "deer camp eggs."

Deer camp eggs are basically scrambled eggs cooked in a cast-iron skillet with sausage, onions, peppers, and a heaping handful of shredded cheese. They're greasy, cheesy, and loaded with enough calories to keep you warm for hours. We serve them with toast, hash browns, and a side of bacon, because why not?

One morning, my cousin Dave decided to try his hand at making deer camp eggs. He'd had a little too much brandy the night before, and his cooking skills were…questionable. He accidentally set the skillet on fire, sending a plume of smoke into the cabin and setting off the fire alarm.

"What are you doing, Dave?" I yelled, trying not to laugh.

"Making it extra crispy!" he replied, grinning like a fool.

We spent the rest of the morning airing out the cabin and scraping burnt eggs off the skillet. But despite the chaos, we all agreed it was the best breakfast we'd ever had—mostly because we were too hungry to care.

The First Buck

For many Wisconsinites, hunting season isn't just a pastime—it's a family tradition that's passed down from generation to generation. The day you bag your first buck is a rite of passage, a moment of pride, and the start of a lifetime of hunting stories.

I remember the day my son, Tyler, got his first buck. He was fourteen, and we'd been sitting in our deer stand for what felt like hours, waiting for any sign of movement. Tyler was fidgety, checking his phone every five minutes and complaining about the cold.

"Patience, Tyler," I said, trying to sound wise and fatherly. "Hunting is all about patience."

He rolled his eyes, clearly not convinced. But then, just as he was about to give up, a young buck stepped out of the trees, cautiously sniffing the air. Tyler's eyes widened, and he froze.

"There he is," I whispered. "Take your time."

Tyler took a deep breath, raised his rifle, and squeezed the trigger. The buck dropped, and for a moment, there was nothing but silence. Then Tyler turned to me, his face a mix of shock and excitement.

"Did I...did I get him?" he asked.

"You got him," I replied, smiling. "You got your first buck."

We climbed down from the stand, and Tyler walked over to the buck, still in disbelief. I patted him on the back, and he grinned from ear to ear.

"That was awesome," he said.

"Welcome to the club," I replied.

The End of the Season

As hunting season draws to a close, there's a sense of melancholy in the air. The deer stands are taken down, the gear is packed away, and the orange jackets are hung up until next year. But there's also a sense of satisfaction—a feeling of having been part of something bigger than yourself, something rooted in tradition, camaraderie, and the great outdoors.

On the last night of the season, we always gather around the campfire for one final toast. We raise our glasses and share our favorite memories, our best stories, and our most outrageous tall tales. We laugh, we reminisce, and we promise to do it all again next year.

And as the fire crackles and the stars shine overhead, there's a feeling of contentment that can only come from a day well spent in the woods, surrounded by friends, family, and the beauty of Wisconsin.

A Tradition Worth Keeping

Hunting season is more than just a time to bag a buck—it's a time to connect with the people you care about, to unplug from the chaos of everyday life, and to appreciate the natural beauty of the world around you. It's a time to honor old traditions, create new memories, and find joy in the simple things.

So if you ever find yourself in Wisconsin during hunting season, don't be surprised if the towns are empty, the diners are packed with camo-clad hunters, and the air is filled with the sound of hunting stories. It's just part of life here—part of what makes Wisconsin, well, Wisconsin.

And if you're lucky enough to be invited to a hunting camp, take it as an honor. Grab your orange jacket, pack a thermos of coffee, and get ready to experience the hunting season hustle. Just remember to listen to the Deer Report, keep an eye out for reflective vests, and never turn down a plate of deer camp eggs.

Guide to Deer Season in Wisconsin
Bagging a Deer, Surviving Deer Camp, and Keeping Your Sense of Humor

1. **Dress for Success (and Safety)**
   Wear as much blaze orange as possible. We're talking hats, jackets, pants, gloves, and if you've got an orange cheesehead, even better. You don't want to be mistaken for a deer—especially if your Uncle Jerry's the one holding the rifle. Bonus points if you accessorize with a matching blaze orange fanny pack for snacks.

2. **The Early Bird Gets... a Nap**
   Everyone will tell you that the best hunting is at dawn. But let's be honest—half the hunters out there are really just looking for an excuse to nap in a deer stand without being judged. If you catch someone snoring, just nudge them and whisper, *"Saw a big one, but it got away."*

3. **Bring Enough Snacks to Last a Wisconsin Winter**
   The deer stand isn't just a place to hunt; it's basically your personal dining room in the woods. Pack enough beef jerky, cheese sticks, and snacks to survive a blizzard. And if you drop a cheese curd on the ground, the *10-second rule* applies, even if it's been there all morning.

4. **Don't Let the Scent Blocker Go to Your Head**
   You can cover yourself in every scent blocker known to man, but if you have a brat with onions and kraut for breakfast, those deer are going to smell you coming from three counties away. So just lean in and embrace the Eau de Brat.

5. **Practice Your "It Was This Big" Hand Gestures**
   Whether you actually see a deer or not, you need to master the art of telling a story with dramatic hand gestures. The key is to look serious and expand your arms wider every time you retell the story. By the end of the season, the deer you "almost" got should be the size of a

moose.

6. **Master the Art of Deer Camp Gossip**
   Deer camp is more than just hunting—it's like a book club, but with fewer books and more tall tales. Be ready to talk about who missed a shot, who brought the worst snacks, and whether or not Gary's new camo makes him look like a yeti.

7. **Take Time to "Appreciate Nature"**
   Translation: If you don't see any deer, it's totally fine to spend an hour staring at a squirrel that's apparently taunting you. Just don't shoot at it or you'll be known as "that guy" at deer camp for the next 20 years.

8. **Claim Your Stand with a Custom Sign**
   If you're really serious about your spot, put up a sign that says *"Bob's Stand – Enter at Your Own Risk"* or *"Reserved for Trophy Bucks and Legendary Hunters Only."* It's mostly for the guys at camp, but if the deer can read, even better.

9. **Prepare for the Camp Cook's "Famous Chili"**
   There's always someone at deer camp who insists on making their "famous chili." Bring antacids and avoid eye contact if they ask for honest feedback. If it has enough kick to be classified as a weapon, don't say we didn't warn you.

10. **Perfect Your "Deer Call"**
    You don't need a fancy deer call. Just practice your best "Ope!" or "You betcha!" while in the stand. If that doesn't work, try talking about the Packers' playoff chances—it'll either attract deer or at least distract you from the cold.

11. **Don't Forget the Thermos**
    It's not deer season without a thermos full of coffee, cocoa, or
    something *"special"* to keep you warm. Remember: *the ratio of coffee to
    "special ingredient" should increase in direct proportion to how cold it gets.*

12. **Designate a Guy for Blame**
    Every deer camp needs someone to blame when things go wrong.
    Didn't see any deer? Must be Carl's fault for taking the last cheese
    curds. Ran out of firewood? Gary's job was to chop it last night. This
    keeps the group dynamic balanced, and keeps you off the hook.

13. **Know the Deer Season Fashion Rules**
    Blaze orange is a must, but you can still show some style. If you have
    a blaze orange Packers beanie, you're doing it right. Camouflage is for
    your pants, not your coffee cup. And under no circumstances should
    you wear socks with holes—that's bad luck, and Aunt Marge will
    never let you hear the end of it.

14. **Always Look Busy When You Return to Camp**
    If you didn't see any deer, just say you were "scouting." If you fell
    asleep in your stand, claim you were "letting the deer come to you."
    The goal is to always look like you had a plan, even if that plan
    involved a two-hour nap and a sandwich.

15. **Bring a Spare Hunting Story for Emergencies**
    If you've got nothing to show after a long day, it's time to bust out a
    "legendary tale" from past seasons. Every Wisconsinite has one in their
    back pocket. Just remember: the key to a good hunting story is to
    throw in at least one "I swear, I'm not making this up."

16. **Don't Shoot the Decoys**
    This may seem obvious, but there's always someone who tries to bag one of those DNR decoys. If you see a deer that's suspiciously not moving, don't shoot. Instead, say to your buddy, *"Would you look at that majestic creature?"* and walk away before the game warden arrives.

17. **Keep the Deer Stand Rumor Mill Rolling**
    If you see a monster buck that gets away, start a rumor about it at camp. By the end of the week, the entire county should know about *"Big Earl, the elusive 14-pointer that only comes out at dawn when there's a full moon."* Who knows? Maybe next year, Big Earl will actually show up.

18. **Set the Ground Rules for Souvenirs**
    You're going to find things in the woods—old deer antlers, beer cans, a set of keys from 1992. Just remember, the rule is: "If you didn't shoot it or drop it, it's fair game." The best find of the day wins a six-pack of Spotted Cow or the honor of not washing dishes for the week.

19. **Stay Quiet, but Not Too Quiet**
    When hunting, silence is key, but don't take it too far. If you hear someone fart in the stand, don't hold in your laughter or it'll come out as an awkward wheeze. Just laugh quietly, like the professionals do, and blame it on a "moose call."

20. **Remember: It's About the Journey, Not the Trophy**
    Deer season isn't just about bagging a buck—it's about the camaraderie, the tall tales, and the chance to spend a week in the woods away from cell service and reality. So relax, have a cold one, and if you don't see a single deer all week, just remember: *there's always next season, and plenty of excuses to go around.*

CHAPTER 11:
THE ART OF THE BRAT FRY

In Wisconsin, the brat fry is not just a cooking technique—it's a social institution. While other states might gather for barbecues or cookouts, we Wisconsinites proudly host brat fries. It's a ritual that's part culinary skill, part community bonding, and part excuse to drink beer before noon. And like any great Wisconsin tradition, it comes with its own unwritten rules, heated debates, and more than a few tall tales.

The Origins of the Brat Fry

Bratwurst is to Wisconsin what lobster is to Maine or what grits are to the South. But in the Dairy State, we don't just eat brats; we celebrate them. Historically, the brat fry was born out of necessity. German immigrants brought their sausage-making skills to Wisconsin, and with long winters to survive, cooking a few brats on an open flame was practically a matter of survival. It didn't take long for the humble brat to become a symbol of community, camaraderie, and good times.

Step 1: Choose Your Brats Wisely

Not all brats are created equal. Ask any seasoned Wisconsinite, and they'll have a strong opinion about where to get the best bratwurst. You have your Johnsonville loyalists, the die-hard Usinger's fans, and those who will only buy from a specific butcher named Gus, who still makes them by hand. The debates about brats can get almost as heated as discussions about who has the best cheese curds, and let's be clear—nobody wins those debates.

When selecting your brats, consider the following factors:

Fresh vs. Precooked: Fresh brats are the gold standard. They're plump, juicy, and need to be handled with the kind of care usually reserved for newborns. Precooked brats are acceptable in an emergency but are often looked down upon with the same disdain reserved for store-bought kringle.

The Casings: Natural casings are a must. If your brat doesn't have a satisfying snap when you bite into it, you might as well be eating a hot dog.

Step 2: Prepare the Beer Bath

Once you've selected your brats, it's time to prep the beer bath. This is a key step in the brat fry process that separates the casual cook from the culinary artist. A good beer bath requires a large pot, sliced onions, a stick of butter, and, of course, a few cans of your favorite Wisconsin beer. The trick is to simmer the brats in the beer bath—not boil them. Boiling brats is a rookie mistake and a surefire way to overcook them. You want them to relax in the beer, absorbing the flavors like they're at a spa.

The beer you choose is also important. A good, drinkable lager is ideal. If you wouldn't drink it, don't cook your brats in it. And for heaven's sake, don't use a craft beer with a name like "Double-Hopped Funky Unicorn IPA." A brat fry is not the time to get experimental.

Step 3: The Grillmaster's Stance

Grilling brats is both a science and an art. First, ensure your grill is hot but not too hot—you're aiming for medium heat, like a polite Midwesterner's enthusiasm. Your goal is to create a caramelized, golden-brown exterior without splitting the casing. Nothing ruins a brat fry faster than brats that resemble overcooked sausages from a gas station roller grill.

The grillmaster's stance is key to achieving perfection. Stand with one hand on your hip, the other holding a beer or a pair of tongs. You should occasionally nod approvingly at the brats, as if you're contemplating life's great mysteries. Flip each brat individually, giving them the care and attention they deserve. This isn't a race—it's a courtship.

Step 4: Assembly and Accompaniments

Once your brats are grilled to perfection, it's time for the final steps: assembly and condiments. In Wisconsin, you serve your brats on a classic brat bun—none of that fancy brioche nonsense. The bun should be sturdy enough to hold the brat, yet soft enough to soak up the juices. Toasting the buns on the grill is encouraged and might earn you the respect of onlookers.

When it comes to toppings, less is more. Purists argue that the only acceptable toppings are sliced onions from the beer bath and a generous squirt of spicy brown mustard. However, some renegades might insist on sauerkraut, which is acceptable but should not be done lightly. Ketchup is strictly forbidden. If you see someone reach for the ketchup bottle, it's your duty as a Wisconsinite to gently intervene with an "Ope, not on the brats, there."

Step 5: The Social Aspect

The brat fry is as much about the social experience as it is about the food. You'll want to have a selection of lawn chairs arranged in a semicircle around the grill. This creates a conversational atmosphere where you can swap stories, complain about the latest road construction, and debate the Packers' season prospects. Everyone should have a drink in hand, even if it's just a can of Sprecher root beer for the designated drivers and kids.

It's also traditional to include a healthy amount of good-natured grilling commentary. Expect phrases like, "You gonna flip those brats again, or are you waiting for them to turn into jerky?" and "You know, back in the day, we didn't use all these fancy grill thermometers."

Step 6: The Sides and Extras

A proper brat fry isn't complete without some traditional Wisconsin sides. Potato salad, baked beans, and coleslaw are standard, but if you want to really impress, whip up a batch of German-style potato salad with bacon. It's an unspoken rule that there should always be more sides than actual space on your plate.

Cheese curds make an excellent appetizer, but be prepared to defend your stash from anyone who claims they need a taste test. Remember, fresh cheese curds should squeak when bitten, which is essentially a badge of quality in Wisconsin.

The Final Step: Post-Brat Fry Rituals

When the brat fry is over, and everyone has eaten their fill, it's customary to stand around the grill and discuss how perfectly the brats were cooked. This is followed by a chorus of "Good job, grillmaster!" and "Those were the best brats I've ever had," even if they were only slightly above average.

Afterward, the grillmaster has the right to first dibs on any remaining beer, and it's understood that the next time someone mentions a cookout, you'll be the first to volunteer your services. After all, in Wisconsin, grilling isn't just cooking—it's an art form, a way of life, and a chance to bring people together one perfectly grilled brat at a time.

So the next time you find yourself grilling in a snowstorm or debating the merits of various brat brands, just remember: the art of the brat fry is more than just sizzling sausage—it's the glue that holds the state together. And if you're doing it right, you'll leave with a full stomach, a new friend, and at least one story worth telling.

Wisconsin-Style Brats: The Ultimate Backyard Recipe

With a Dash of Humor and a Lot of Beer

When it comes to cooking brats, you're not just making food—you're upholding a Wisconsin tradition. This isn't a meal; it's a declaration of your loyalty to the Dairy State. Follow this recipe, add in a few laughs, and you'll have brats so good, even the neighbors will show up uninvited (again).

Ingredients:

- ❖ **10 fresh bratwurst sausages** (because you don't cook just a few brats in Wisconsin—what if Cousin Larry stops by?)
- ❖ **1 large onion, sliced** (to prove you eat vegetables)
- ❖ **3 cans of beer** (local, if possible—Spotted Cow, Miller, or any beer that proudly proclaims "Brewed in Wisconsin")
- ❖ **1 stick of butter** (yes, the whole stick—it's called "flavor insurance")
- ❖ **A couple of cloves of garlic, minced** (to keep the vampires and Minnesotans away)
- ❖ **Pretzel buns** (because if you're not getting carbs from multiple angles, are you really even trying?)
- ❖ **Spicy brown mustard** (not optional)
- ❖ **Sauerkraut** (only if you don't mind your breath smelling like victory)
- ❖ **Cheese slices** (because you're in Wisconsin, and putting cheese on a brat is basically the law)

Instructions:

Step 1: Get the Beer Bath Ready

- In a large pot (the kind you've had since your wedding or found at a rummage sale), toss in your **sliced onions, butter, minced garlic,** and **three cans of beer**. If you're feeling fancy, save a sip of the beer for yourself while you work—it's called a "chef's tax."
- Bring this glorious concoction to a simmer. When your kitchen starts smelling like the state fair, you're doing it right.

Step 2: Simmer the Brats

- Add your **bratwursts** to the beer bath, gently reminding them that they're about to fulfill their life's purpose. Let the brats simmer for about **15 minutes**, but don't let them boil. You want them hot-tub relaxed, not *waterpark wild.*

- Stir occasionally, but don't get too carried away—it's brats, not a risotto. While simmering, remember to open another beer for yourself, because it's important to stay hydrated during this strenuous cooking process.

Step 3: Fire Up the Grill

- Once the brats are done relaxing in their beer sauna, it's time to transfer them to the grill. If you don't have a grill, find a friend who does, or question your life choices as a Wisconsinite.
- Preheat your grill to **medium-high heat**, or until it feels like an August day at the county fair. Place the brats on the grill, turning them gently and often. Your goal here is to get those **perfect grill marks**—it's not just cooking, it's creating art.
- While grilling, avoid the temptation to poke or stab the brats. They're not balloons at a kid's birthday party, and all that juicy goodness deserves to stay inside.

Step 4: Grill the Onions Too

- While the brats are working on their tans, toss those **beer-butter onions** on a piece of foil on the grill. Let them cook until they're slightly caramelized and smell like they could solve all of life's problems. Don't forget to stir them once or twice—this step is more about making you look busy than actually improving the flavor.

Step 5: Assemble Like a Pro

- Grab your **pretzel buns** and give them a quick toast on the grill. Not enough to set off the smoke alarm, but enough to make them think they're at a luxury spa.
- Place a brat in each bun, add a scoop of the **grilled onions**, a generous squirt of **spicy brown mustard**, and a handful of **sauerkraut** (if you're into that sort of thing).
- If you really want to impress the in-laws, add a slice of **cheese**—Colby Jack, sharp cheddar, or anything that makes your arteries preemptively groan.

Pro Tips for Brat Excellence:

- **Don't Rush the Process**: Brats are like friendships—they're best when given time to develop. Don't rush the grilling, and don't skip the beer bath. It's basically mandatory in Wisconsin law.

- **Have Plenty of Beer on Hand**: For drinking, simmering, and socializing. If anyone complains about the beer choice, remind them that in Wisconsin, every beer is the right beer.
- **Have an Excuse Ready for Why You Made So Many**: When you inevitably have extra brats, just say, *"Well, you never know who might show up!"* If anyone questions this, just stare into the distance like you're expecting a parade.
- **Deflect All Compliments with a Casual Shrug**: If someone says these are the best brats they've ever had, don't brag. Just smile, shrug, and say, *"Ah, they're just brats."* (Even though deep down, you know you've achieved bratwurst nirvana.)

Serving Suggestions:

- **Potato Salad**: It's not mandatory, but it will make your grandma proud.
- **More Cheese**: Again, it's the law. Cheese curds on the side are basically a requirement.
- **Chips**: Grab a big bag of local favorites and let everyone complain that they can't stop eating them.
- **Beer**: Serve with another cold beer, because this is Wisconsin and "water" isn't part of our vocabulary during a cookout.

Final Step: Enjoy!

Congratulations, you've just made Wisconsin-style brats that will make you the hero of the backyard. Serve them up, kick back, and wait for the inevitable *"What's your secret?"* questions. Just smile and say, *"Oh, you know, a little love and a lot of beer."* Then lean back and bask in the glory of being the **Brat Master**.

And remember: in Wisconsin, it's not just a cookout—it's a way of life.

CHAPTER 12:
THE LEGEND OF KRINGLE AND OTHER SWEET TREATS

If there's one thing Wisconsinites know how to do, it's eat. And while we love our cheese, brats, and beer, we've also got a serious sweet tooth. Now, you can keep your fancy French pastries and artisanal cakes—we'll take a freshly baked kringle or a batch of homemade bars any day of the week. Desserts in Wisconsin aren't about being fancy; they're about being delicious. And nothing embodies that better than our unofficial state pastry: the kringle.

For those of you who aren't familiar with it, a kringle is a flaky, buttery, ring-shaped pastry filled with everything from almond paste to cherries to pecans. It's Danish in origin, but somewhere along the way, Wisconsin adopted it, perfected it, and turned it into a local legend. Around here, kringle isn't just a pastry—it's a way of life.

The Kringle Connection

The town of Racine is known as the "Kringle Capital of the World," and for good reason. There are more bakeries per capita in Racine than there are bars in Milwaukee (and that's saying something). People come from miles around to get their hands on a fresh kringle, and Racine's bakeries are more than happy to oblige.

My family has a long-standing tradition of picking up a kringle from O&H Danish Bakery every time we pass through Racine. It doesn't matter if we're on our way to a family reunion, a wedding, or a doctor's appointment—if we're within ten miles of O&H, we're stopping for kringle. And heaven help you if you forget to bring one home. My mom once went to Racine for a conference and came back empty-handed. My dad didn't speak to her for three days.

Of course, everyone's got their favorite kringle flavor. My mom loves the almond kringle, my wife is partial to the cherry cheese, and my dad swears by the pecan. Personally, I'm a fan of the raspberry kringle—there's something about the combination of sweet raspberry filling and flaky pastry that just hits the spot.

The Kringle Feud

Now, you might think that a town full of bakeries would be one big happy family. But in Racine, there's a quiet, ongoing feud between the major kringle bakeries. O&H and Larsen's Bakery are the main contenders, each with its own loyal following and each claiming to have the best kringle in town. It's a rivalry that's been simmering for decades, and while it's mostly good-natured, there's definitely some tension.

One time, I made the mistake of bringing a kringle from O&H to a family gathering on my wife's side. I thought I was being thoughtful, but apparently, her uncle Bob is a die-hard Larsen's fan. When he saw the O&H box, he narrowed his eyes and muttered, "O&H, huh? Well, I guess it's better than nothing."

The rest of the family laughed, but I could tell he wasn't joking. He picked at his slice of kringle like it was a day-old donut, and every now and then, he'd glance at me like I'd personally insulted his taste in pastries. After that, I made sure to ask about bakery preferences before showing up with a kringle.

The Mystery of the State Fair Cream Puff

While kringle reigns supreme in Racine, there's another dessert that holds a special place in the hearts of Wisconsinites: the State Fair cream puff. For those of you who've never experienced it, the cream puff is a giant, flaky pastry filled with mountains of whipped cream. It's messy, it's indulgent, and it's absolutely glorious.

The Wisconsin State Fair sells tens of thousands of cream puffs every year, and people line up for hours to get their hands on one. It's a tradition, a rite of passage, and a badge of honor. But the real mystery isn't why people love cream puffs so much—it's how they manage to eat them without ending up covered in whipped cream.

I've tried every technique in the book—splitting the cream puff in half, eating it like a sandwich, even using a fork and knife (don't judge me). But no matter what I do, I always end up with whipped cream on my nose and powdered sugar in my hair. It's just part of the experience.

One year, I saw a couple at the State Fair sharing a cream puff in perfect harmony. They each took small, delicate bites, never spilling a drop of whipped cream. It was like watching a ballet, and I was in awe. I asked them how they did it, and the woman just smiled and said, "It's all about teamwork."

My wife and I tried to replicate their technique the following year, but it ended with me getting a face full of whipped cream and her laughing so hard she could barely breathe. We decided to stick to our usual strategy of eating separately and meeting up for hand sanitizer afterwards.

Bars and Other Sweet Delights

If there's one dessert that's as ubiquitous as kringle in Wisconsin, it's bars. I'm not talking about the kind where you get a beer—I'm talking about the sweet, square-shaped desserts that every Wisconsinite's grandma has a recipe for. There are lemon bars, scotcheroos, chocolate revel bars, seven-layer bars, and a dozen other varieties. And no matter what kind of potluck, church supper, or family gathering you're at, you're guaranteed to find a pan of bars on the dessert table.

My grandma's specialty was rhubarb bars—a sweet-tart concoction with a buttery crust and a layer of rhubarb filling. She made them every summer with rhubarb from her garden, and they were always a hit. I remember sitting in her kitchen, watching her chop the rhubarb with the precision of a surgeon and measuring out just the right amount of sugar to balance the tartness.

Grandma never wrote down her recipe—it was all in her head. But one summer, I convinced her to let me write it down as she made the bars. I followed her around the kitchen with a notepad, scribbling down her instructions and measurements. When I was done, I proudly showed her the recipe, expecting her to be impressed.

She glanced at it, nodded, and said, "Looks good, but you didn't write down the most important step."

"What's that?" I asked.

"Don't forget to add love," she replied, winking at me.

The Dairy Delights

No discussion of Wisconsin desserts would be complete without mentioning our dairy delights. After all, we're the Dairy State, and we take our ice cream, custard, and cheese curds very seriously. If you're ever in Wisconsin, you owe it to yourself to stop at a dairy stand and try a fresh scoop of ice cream or a deep-fried cheese curd. It's the closest thing to heaven you'll find on this side of the Mississippi.

One of my favorite spots is Babcock Hall Dairy Store in Madison. They've got flavors you won't find anywhere else, like Orange Custard Chocolate Chip and Union Utopia. But my personal favorite is the Badger Blast, a chocolate ice cream with chocolate chunks and swirls of fudge. It's rich, decadent, and worth every calorie.

I once made the mistake of ordering a double scoop of Badger Blast on a hot summer day. The ice cream started melting faster than I could eat it, and before I knew it, I had chocolate running down my arm and dripping onto my shoes. My wife handed me a stack of napkins and said, "You need to work on your ice cream technique."

"I'm doing my best," I replied, wiping chocolate off my elbow.

The Great Pie Debate

Of course, no discussion of Wisconsin desserts would be complete without addressing the great pie debate. Specifically, the question of whether apple pie or pumpkin pie is the superior fall dessert. It's a debate that divides families, strains friendships, and can turn a peaceful Thanksgiving dinner into a heated argument.

Personally, I'm an apple pie guy. There's something about a warm slice of apple pie with a scoop of vanilla ice cream that just can't be beat. But my wife is firmly in the pumpkin pie camp, and she's not shy about expressing her opinion.

"Apple pie is fine," she says, "but pumpkin pie has that warm, spicy flavor that just tastes like fall."

"Apple pie is fall," I counter. "It's got apples, cinnamon, and a buttery crust. What more do you need?"

"Nutmeg," she replies, raising an eyebrow.

In the end, we usually end up making both pies for Thanksgiving, which is probably for the best. After all, there's no such thing as too much pie.

Sweet Memories

For me, Wisconsin desserts aren't just about the taste—they're about the memories. They're about sitting in my grandma's kitchen, watching her bake rhubarb bars with a smile on her face. They're about sharing a cream puff with my wife at the State Fair, laughing as we both end up covered in whipped cream. They're about picking up a kringle from O&H and knowing that I'm bringing home more than just a pastry—I'm bringing home a piece of Wisconsin.

In the end, it's not just the desserts that make Wisconsin special—it's the people, the traditions, and the stories that come with them. Whether it's a kringle feud, a cream puff catastrophe, or a bar recipe passed down through generations, these sweet treats are a reminder of everything we hold dear: family, community, and the simple joys of life.

So the next time you find yourself in Wisconsin, don't just settle for a donut or a cupcake. Take a detour to Racine for a kringle, stop at a dairy stand for a scoop of ice cream, and pick up a batch of bars from the church bake sale. And if you ever get the chance to try a State Fair cream puff, take it—just make sure you've got plenty of napkins.

The Legend of the Magic Kringle: A Short Story

In the small town of Sturbridge, Wisconsin, the locals took pride in three things: cheese, the Packers, and the legendary Nielsen's Kringle Haus. Every Christmas Eve, the bakery unveiled a special Magic Kringle, said to bring good luck for a year to the person who found the hidden golden almond within.

Gunnar Nielsen, the bakery's owner, was known for his precise baking skills. This year, after a disastrous previous year where a snowstorm ruined the Magic Kringle, Gunnar decided to add a twist—he hid a small golden almond in the massive pastry. Whoever found it would supposedly be blessed with good fortune. His loyal employee, Mildred, watched nervously as he prepared the kringle.

"Are you sure about this, Gunnar?" she asked.

"After last year's disaster, we could use some luck," Gunnar replied with a grin.

That evening, the townspeople gathered outside the bakery. Gunnar brought out the enormous kringle, placing it on a long wooden table. The crowd buzzed with excitement.

"There's a golden almond hidden somewhere in this kringle," Gunnar announced. "The person who finds it will have a year of good luck!"

Little Timmy Thompson got the first slice but came up empty-handed. More people lined up to try their luck, but each slice seemed devoid of the elusive almond. As the line dwindled, anticipation grew. Rumors began to spread—had Gunnar hidden it too well, or was there even an almond at all?

Mildred, who'd been a part of this tradition for decades, took her slice. She bit into it, only to find it almond-free. With each failed attempt, the tension increased. Gunnar nervously wondered if he had indeed buried the almond too deeply.

At the back of the line, old Mrs. Jorgensen finally reached the table. She was well into her nineties and had been baking kringles long before the Nielsen family. Gunnar handed her the last slice, hoping for a miracle.

Mrs. Jorgensen inspected her piece with trembling hands and took a small bite. The crowd held its breath. After a long pause, Mrs. Jorgensen slowly reached into her mouth and pulled out her hand, revealing the golden almond.

The townspeople erupted into cheers and applause. Mrs. Jorgensen raised the almond triumphantly, her face glowing with joy. Gunnar sighed in relief, and even Mildred wiped away a tear.

From that day forward, Mrs. Jorgensen's luck turned around. She won the church raffle multiple times, her tomatoes won blue ribbons, and her mischievous cat finally stopped knocking over her flowerpots.

As for Nielsen's Kringle Haus, business boomed, and the bakery became a must-visit destination for travelers and locals alike. Gunnar's Magic Kringle became the stuff of legend, and every Christmas Eve, people gathered in hopes of finding the golden almond and a bit of Wisconsin magic.

No matter how many almonds were found, one thing was certain: there's nothing more magical than a little bit of luck, a lot of butter, and a kringle shared with friends.

The End

CHAPTER 13:
"OPE!" AND OTHER WISCONSIN VOCABULARY

Every region has its own language—those little words and phrases that mark you as a local and leave outsiders scratching their heads. Here in Wisconsin, we've got our own unique way of speaking, complete with slang, expressions, and a whole lot of friendly politeness. Some call it "Midwestern Nice," but I like to think of it as Wisconsinese—the unofficial language of the Badger State.

If you've spent any time in Wisconsin, you've probably heard people say things like "bubbler," "you betcha," and "Uff da!" But there's one word that defines Wisconsin more than any other: "Ope!" It's the sound you make when you accidentally bump into someone, drop something, or need to sneak past a group of people in a crowded room. "Ope" isn't just a word—it's a lifestyle.

The Meaning of "Ope"

For those of you who aren't familiar with it, "Ope" is a versatile little word that can mean just about anything. It's an expression of surprise, an apology, and a way to diffuse awkward situations. It's like saying "Oops," but with more Midwest charm. And once you start saying it, you can't stop.

Imagine this: you're walking down the grocery store aisle, pushing your cart, when you accidentally bump into someone. What do you say? "Ope, sorry 'bout that!" Or maybe you're trying to squeeze past someone in a crowded room. What do you say? "Ope, lemme just sneak past ya there!" And if you drop your keys while fumbling with your car door? "Ope, got 'em!"

One time, I was helping my neighbor Gary move some furniture, and I accidentally knocked over a lamp. Without thinking, I said, "Ope, didn't mean to do that!" Gary just chuckled and said, "You sound like my Aunt Marge."

I realized then that "Ope" is more than just a word—it's part of our cultural DNA. It's a reflex, a way of acknowledging our mistakes while maintaining our politeness. And in a state known for its friendliness, "Ope" is the ultimate expression of Wisconsin Nice.

The Bubbler Debate

If you ever want to start a heated debate in Wisconsin, just ask people what they call the thing you drink water from in public buildings. Most of the country calls it a "water fountain," but here in Wisconsin, we call it a "bubbler." And if you dare to suggest otherwise, you'd better be prepared to defend yourself.

The origin of the word "bubbler" dates back to the early 1900s, when a company called Kohler began manufacturing a drinking fountain that bubbled water from the spout instead of shooting it in a stream. The name stuck, and to this day, Wisconsinites proudly refer to drinking fountains as bubblers.

Of course, this leads to a lot of confusion for outsiders. I once had a friend from Illinois visit, and when I pointed out the bubbler in the hallway, he looked at me like I was speaking another language.

"What's a bubbler?" he asked, genuinely puzzled.

"It's a drinking fountain," I replied.

"Then why don't you just call it a drinking fountain?" he countered.

"Because it's a bubbler," I said, as if that explained everything.

We went back and forth for a while, but in the end, we agreed to disagree. He kept calling it a drinking fountain, and I kept calling it a bubbler. But deep down, I knew I was right.

Uff Da and Other Exclamations

One of the great things about Wisconsin is that we're not afraid to show our emotions—especially when those emotions can be summed up with a simple exclamation. And one of the most iconic exclamations in Wisconsin is "Uff da!" It's a phrase of Norwegian origin that's used to express surprise, exhaustion, or mild frustration. Think of it as the Scandinavian equivalent of saying, "Oh, boy" or "Good grief."

For example, if you're carrying a heavy load of groceries and the bottom of the bag breaks, you might say, "Uff da!" Or if you hear that the Packers lost to the Bears (again), you might let out a weary, "Uff da!" It's a way of venting your frustration without resorting to stronger language, and it's a phrase that every Wisconsinite understands instinctively.

Other regional exclamations include "For cryin' out loud," which is used to express mild annoyance, and "Holy cow!" which is reserved for moments of genuine surprise. And if you ever hear someone say "Jeez Louise," you know they've reached their limit.

One of my favorite expressions comes from my grandpa, who used to say "Well, I'll be dipped in buttermilk" whenever he was genuinely astonished by something. I have no idea where that phrase came from, but it never failed to make me laugh.

Midwest Politeness

Here in Wisconsin, we take politeness very seriously. If you're at the grocery store and someone lets you cut in line, you're expected to say "Thanks a million" or "Much obliged." If someone does you a favor, you'd better respond with "I appreciate it" or "You're a lifesaver." And if you bump into someone, you say "Ope, sorry 'bout that"—even if it wasn't your fault.

One time, I was at a family reunion, and my cousin Dave accidentally spilled a pitcher of lemonade all over me. He turned bright red and immediately started apologizing.

"Ope, sorry, Wayne!" he stammered. "I didn't see you standing there!"

"No worries, Dave," I replied, brushing off the lemonade. "Guess I'll be extra sweet now."

Dave laughed nervously, and my Aunt Marge handed me a towel. "You boys and your 'opes,'" she said, shaking her head. "You're gonna wear that word out one of these days."

"You Betcha" and Other Affirmations

When it comes to expressing agreement in Wisconsin, there are plenty of options. You could say "Yeah, sure," "Absolutely," or "Of course," but none of those quite capture the Midwestern spirit like "You betcha." It's a phrase that conveys not just agreement, but enthusiasm and a sense of camaraderie.

For example, if someone asks you if you're going to the Friday night fish fry, you might respond with "You betcha!" If they ask if you want another beer, you could say "Oh, you betcha!" And if someone suggests that the Packers have a good chance of making it to the playoffs, you'd respond with "You betcha—go Pack go!"

Another classic Wisconsin affirmation is "Don'tcha know," which is often used to emphasize a point or add a touch of folksy wisdom to a statement. For example, you might say, "It's gonna be a long winter, don'tcha know" or "You gotta keep the grill hot, don'tcha know." It's a way of connecting with others and showing that you're all on the same page.

And if you ever find yourself agreeing to something with a simple "Yeah, sure" or "Okay," don't be surprised if someone responds with, "Well, ain't that just the truth!" It's the Wisconsin way of acknowledging that you've said something wise, even if it was completely obvious.

Navigating the Language of Hospitality

One of the defining characteristics of Wisconsinese is our focus on hospitality. We like to make people feel welcome, whether they're family, friends, or complete strangers. And part of that hospitality is offering food and drink to anyone who steps foot in our homes.

If you're visiting someone's house in Wisconsin, you can expect to hear phrases like "Can I getcha something to eat?" or "How 'bout a drink?" And even if you decline, they'll probably insist. It's considered rude to let a guest go hungry or thirsty, and we take that very seriously.

My Aunt Marge is a prime example of this. No matter what time of day you visit, she's always ready with a plate of cookies, a cup of coffee, or a bowl of hot dish. And if you dare to refuse, she'll look at you with a mix of confusion and disappointment.

"Are you sure?" she'll ask. "I've got plenty."

"Really, I'm fine," you'll reply.

"Well, if you change your mind, don't be shy," she'll say, eyeing you like she's just waiting for you to cave.

The Final Word

In the end, Wisconsinese is more than just a collection of words and phrases—it's a reflection of who we are as a people. It's about politeness, hospitality, and a deep sense of community. It's about finding the humor in life's little mishaps and expressing your emotions without making a fuss. And most of all, it's about making sure everyone feels welcome, whether they're from here or just passing through.

So the next time you find yourself in Wisconsin, don't be surprised if you hear someone say "Ope!" or ask you if you want a drink from the bubbler. And if someone offers you a slice of kringle, a cold beer, or a spot at the Friday night fish fry, just smile and say "You betcha!" After all, that's the Wisconsin way.

A Wisconsinite's Glossary

For all the out-of-towners trying to keep up

Ope (exclamation)
The universal Wisconsin word used when bumping into someone, dropping something, or finding oneself in a mildly awkward situation. Usually followed by "sorry 'bout that" or "lemme just squeeze past ya."

Bubbler (noun)
What most of the world calls a drinking fountain. In Wisconsin, it's the thing you drink water from, not something that makes bubbles in your hot tub.

Up North (noun)
A mythical place that technically starts anywhere 50 miles north of where you currently are. It's where people escape for long weekends, fishing trips, and the occasional bear sighting.

Squeaky (adjective)
The proper state of a **cheese curd**. If it doesn't squeak against your teeth, it's either not fresh or from out of state.

The Pack (noun)
Short for the **Green Bay Packers**. Referring to the team by anything else, such as "Green Bay" or "the football team," will instantly mark you as an outsider.

Supper Club (noun)
A traditional Wisconsin dining establishment known for serving prime rib, fish fry, and brandy Old Fashioneds. It's not a fancy club you need to join, but it's definitely a place you should go.

Brandy Old Fashioned (noun)
The state drink of Wisconsin. Made with brandy, muddled fruit, bitters, and usually ordered "sweet" (with 7-Up) or "sour" (with Squirt). Do not order it with bourbon if you value your reputation.

Polka (noun)
A type of lively dance music that's part of every Wisconsin wedding and festival. Even if you claim you don't know how to polka, your feet will automatically start moving when you hear it.

FIB (noun)
An acronym that stands for "Friendly Illinois Buddy." It's what Wisconsinites sometimes call Illinois drivers… when they're being sarcastic.

Deer Camp (noun)
The sacred place where Wisconsin hunters gather for a week each November. Known for its rustic cabins, strong opinions on camo patterns, and arguments over the best way to cook venison.

Kwik Trip (noun)
A convenience store that's more beloved than some family members. It's where you stop for coffee, Glazers, and essential life supplies (like 30-packs of beer). Never insult Kwik Trip—ever.

Fish Fry (noun)
A Friday night institution involving fried fish (usually cod, perch, or walleye), potato pancakes, coleslaw, and rye bread. It's where the entire town gathers to eat and gossip.

Cripes (exclamation)
An expression of mild frustration or surprise. Often used when someone's team fumbles the football or when you burn the brats.

Hotdish (noun)
The Midwest version of a casserole, typically involving tater tots, ground beef, and a creamy soup base. Don't try to outdo Aunt Marge's recipe—it's impossible.

Schnecks (noun)
A type of sweet roll you get at a bakery. Not to be confused with donuts, even though they serve the same purpose of making mornings worth waking up for.

Sconnie (noun/adjective)
A term for a true Wisconsinite or anything related to Wisconsin. For example, "He's a real Sconnie" or "That's some Sconnie behavior, grilling in the snow like that."

The Dells (noun)
Short for **Wisconsin Dells**, the waterpark capital of the world. Even if you've only been there once, you'll tell every out-of-towner about it like you go every summer.

Frozen Tundra (noun)
What Wisconsinites call **Lambeau Field** in the dead of winter. It's also an expression of pride, as in "He's tough enough to survive the Frozen Tundra."

Snowmobile (noun/verb)
A winter recreational vehicle that also doubles as an acceptable mode of transportation during heavy snow. For example, "Just gonna snowmobile over to Dave's place—roads are a mess."

Ya Der Hey (exclamation)
An all-purpose phrase that roughly means "Yes, of course!" or "I agree!" Often heard when confirming plans or when someone offers you another beer.

Chapter 14:
The Lambeau Leap of Faith

If there's one thing that binds all Wisconsinites together, it's our undying love for the Green Bay Packers. It doesn't matter if you live in Milwaukee, Madison, or Manitowoc—if you're from Wisconsin, you're a Packers fan. And if you're not, well…let's just say you keep that information to yourself. The Packers aren't just a football team—they're a religion. And Lambeau Field isn't just a stadium—it's a sacred place where we gather to worship at the altar of Vince Lombardi, cheese curds, and Lambeau Leaps.

The Lambeau Leap is more than just a touchdown celebration—it's a rite of passage, a symbol of triumph, and a moment of pure, unfiltered joy. Watching a Packer leap into the stands, greeted by a sea of fans cheering and hugging like long-lost family members, it's impossible not to get caught up in the excitement. It's a move that says, "We did it!"—and it's a move that every Packer fan dreams of experiencing, at least once in their life.

The First Lambeau Experience

My first time at Lambeau Field was a day I'll never forget. I was ten years old, and my dad had finally decided I was old enough to handle the freezing temperatures and the "grown-up words" that occasionally fly around in the stands. We bundled up in layers of green and gold, packed a thermos of hot chocolate, and made the drive to Green Bay, listening to the pre-game show on the radio the whole way there.

When we pulled into the parking lot, it was like stepping into a different world. Everywhere I looked, there were people grilling brats, waving Packers flags, and tossing footballs in the snow. The air smelled like a mix of charcoal, beer, and hope. My dad handed me a foam cheesehead, and I wore it with the pride of a knight donning his armor.

As we walked up to the stadium, I could hear the roar of the crowd and the chant of "Go Pack Go!" echoing through the halls. And when we stepped into the stands, and I saw the field for the first time, I knew I was part of something special.

That day, I witnessed my first Lambeau Leap. The Packers were down by a touchdown, but after a long drive, Brett Favre launched a pass into the end zone, and the receiver made a diving catch for the score. The crowd erupted in cheers, and the player leaped into the stands, disappearing into a sea of green and gold. I remember watching, wide-eyed, as the fans hugged him, patted him on the back, and chanted his name.

"That's the Lambeau Leap," my dad said, smiling. "Maybe one day you'll get to do it."

I laughed, but deep down, I wondered if he was right.

The Tailgate Tradition

Of course, no trip to Lambeau is complete without a tailgate. Tailgating at Lambeau is an art form, perfected over generations of Packer fans who know that the only thing better than watching the game is eating brats and drinking beer before the game. It's not just a pre-game ritual—it's a social event, a chance to catch up with old friends, make new ones, and bond over your shared love of football and grilled meat.

The key to a successful tailgate is preparation. You need a sturdy grill, plenty of folding chairs, and enough bratwurst to feed a small army. And don't forget the cheese curds—they're a must-have snack, especially when you're standing around in the cold, waiting for the game to start.

My buddy Carl takes his tailgating very seriously. He's got a checklist that includes everything from condiments to backup propane tanks. One year, he even brought a portable deep fryer so he could make cheese curds on the spot. He set up a folding table, filled the fryer with oil, and started frying up curds like a pro.

"You want some?" he asked, holding out a basket of golden, crispy cheese curds.

"Of course," I replied, grabbing a handful. "You know, you're spoiling me for regular tailgating."

Carl grinned. "That's the idea."

The "Frozen Tundra" Challenge

There's a reason Lambeau Field is known as the "Frozen Tundra." Winters in Wisconsin are no joke, and if you're going to a game at Lambeau in December or January, you'd better be prepared for freezing temperatures, bone-chilling winds, and the possibility of a snowstorm. But that's all part of the experience. If you're not willing to brave the cold, are you even a real Packers fan?

My dad always used to say, "There's no such thing as bad weather—just bad clothing." And he took that philosophy to heart. Whenever we went to a game in the winter, he made sure we were dressed like Arctic explorers. Thermal socks, long underwear, fleece-lined gloves—you name it, we wore it. We looked like we were about to climb Mount Everest, but at least we stayed warm.

One year, we went to a game in late December, and the temperature was well below zero. The wind chill made it feel even colder, and by halftime, I couldn't feel my toes. I looked over at my dad, expecting him to suggest we head inside to warm up, but he just smiled and handed me a cup of hot chocolate.

"Hang in there, buddy," he said. "It's part of the experience."

And he was right. As miserable as the cold was, there was something exhilarating about being out there, cheering for the Packers in the snow. It was a badge of honor, a testament to our dedication. And when the Packers scored a touchdown and the player leaped into the stands, it made it all worth it.

The Lambeau Faithful

One of the things that makes Lambeau Field so special is the fans. Packers fans aren't just spectators—they're part of the team, part of the tradition, and part of the reason Lambeau is such an intimidating place for visiting teams. The fans are loud, loyal, and fiercely protective of their team and their stadium.

And despite the cold, the crowds at Lambeau are always warm and welcoming. I've been to games where I've shared hot chocolate with strangers, swapped stories with fans from out of state, and even exchanged recipes for venison chili with a guy in the row behind me. It's like one big family reunion, except everyone's wearing green and gold.

One of my favorite Lambeau memories is from a game against the Bears. The Packers were losing, and the mood in the stands was tense. But then, in the fourth quarter, the Packers mounted a comeback and took the lead. The crowd went wild, and when the Bears fumbled on their final drive, sealing the victory, the noise was deafening.

As we celebrated, I looked over at the guy next to me—a complete stranger who was grinning from ear to ear. Without a word, we hugged, jumping up and down like we'd just won the lottery. And in a way, we had.

The Lambeau Leap of Faith

As much as I love watching the Lambeau Leap, I never thought I'd get the chance to experience it myself. But one summer, I got an invitation to a charity event at Lambeau Field. It was a fundraiser for the Packers Foundation, and part of the event included the opportunity to run onto the field and attempt a Lambeau Leap.

When I got the invitation, I couldn't believe it. I called my dad and told him the news, and he laughed and said, "Well, I guess it's time for your leap of faith."

On the day of the event, I was nervous. I wasn't sure if I could actually make the leap—after all, those walls are higher than they look on TV. But as I stood on the field, looking up at the stands, I felt a surge of adrenaline. This was my chance to be part of the tradition, to experience the joy and excitement of a Lambeau Leap.

When it was my turn, I took a deep breath, ran towards the wall, and jumped. For a moment, I felt weightless, like I was floating. And then, to my amazement, I felt hands grabbing me and pulling me up. I'd made it.

As I stood there, surrounded by cheering fans and feeling like I was on top of the world, I couldn't help but laugh. I'd done it. I'd taken the leap, and I'd made it.

The Lasting Legacy

The Lambeau Leap isn't just a celebration—it's a symbol of unity. It's a moment when players and fans come together, sharing in the joy of a touchdown and the pride of being part of something bigger than themselves. It's a reminder that, in Wisconsin, football is more than just a game—it's a way of life.

And whether you're watching from the stands, grilling brats in the parking lot, or leaping into the arms of fellow fans, you're part of that tradition. You're part of the legacy of Lambeau Field, a place where the past and the present come together in a celebration of everything we love about football, family, and friendship.

So the next time you find yourself at Lambeau Field, take a moment to soak it all in. Listen to the roar of the crowd, feel the chill in the air, and watch as the Packers leap into the stands, greeted by a sea of smiling faces. And if you ever get the chance to attempt your own Lambeau Leap, take it—you won't regret it.

Packers Jokes for Every Cheesehead

For when the game's on and the beer is flowing

Why don't the Packers play poker?
Because they can't find a dealer that doesn't work for the Bears!

What's a Green Bay Packer's favorite type of music?
Rock and Rodgers.

Why did the football go to Lambeau Field?
It wanted to be kicked around by a professional!

How do you know someone's a Packers fan?
Don't worry, they'll tell you. Loudly. And often.

Why don't the Packers need air conditioning at Lambeau Field?
Because the fans are so cool!

What do you call a Packers fan with half a brain?
Gifted. They put all their brainpower into cheering for the right team.

Why did Aaron Rodgers bring a ladder to Lambeau?
He wanted to reach the top of the NFC North!

What do Packers fans and Wisconsin mosquitoes have in common?
They're both relentless, and they'll find you wherever you go.

Why do Packers fans make terrible secret agents?
Because they can't stop yelling, "Go Pack Go!" at the worst possible moments.

Why did the cheese curd go to the Packers game?
It wanted to join the "cheese" section!

How many Packers fans does it take to change a light bulb?
None—they just cheer in the dark and wait for Aaron Rodgers to light things up.

What's the difference between the Packers and a dollar bill?
You can still get four quarters out of a Packers game!

Why did the football team go to the bakery?
To get their turnovers. (But not the Packers, they're hanging onto those wins!)

Why don't Packers fans do well in math class?
Because every time they hear "division," they think, "NFC North Champs!"

Why did the Lambeau Field groundskeeper bring a dictionary to work?
He wanted to "define the field" before the Packers crushed their opponents.

What do you call a Packers fan at the Super Bowl?
Lucky! We usually watch it at home with a plate of brats and cheese curds.

Why do Packers fans love winter?
Because snow is the only whiteout they can support!

Why did the Packers bring a blanket to the game?
Because they wanted to cover their spread!

Why do Bears fans always root for the Packers?
Because someone's got to show them what a winning team looks like!

Why did the Packers fan eat a candle after the game?
They wanted to celebrate the win with a "light" snack!

Bonus:
How can you tell if a Packers fan is happy?
They're breathing.

Disclaimer: These jokes are all in good fun. If you're at Lambeau, make sure you've got a cheesehead nearby to deflect any incoming tomato throws from rival fans! Go Pack Go!

CHAPTER 15:
PROUDLY WISCONSIN: THE BRANDS WE LOVE

There are certain brands that are more than just companies—they're part of the culture, woven into the very fabric of a place. Here in Wisconsin, we've got plenty of those. Brands that remind us of home, that we take pride in, and that we'll defend to the death against any outsider who dares to suggest something else might be better. From cheese and beer to motorcycles and ice cream, Wisconsin brands aren't just products—they're part of who we are.

The Big Cheese: Wisconsin Dairy

When most people think of Wisconsin, they think of cheese—and for good reason. We're not called the Dairy State for nothing. Wisconsin produces more than 600 varieties of cheese, and we take our cheese seriously. If you ever visit, you'll notice that we don't just eat cheese—we celebrate it. Cheese festivals, cheese curd stands, cheese-themed souvenirs—it's all part of the Wisconsin experience.

And if you want the true Wisconsin cheese experience, you have to try Wisconsin cheese curds. They're not just a side dish—they're a delicacy. Fresh, squeaky cheese curds are a treat in themselves, but if you want to take it to the next level, you can get them deep-fried. If you're at a bar, a county fair, or pretty much any sporting event, chances are you'll find a basket of deep-fried cheese curds on the menu.

Of course, behind every great cheese is a great brand, and in Wisconsin, that brand is often Kraft. Headquartered in Madison, Kraft is the company behind the legendary Velveeta, that golden, gooey cheese product that turns any gathering into a party. Whether you're making nachos, grilled cheese, or the classic Wisconsin dish known as Beer Cheese Soup, Velveeta is a key ingredient.

And let's not forget about Sargento, the family-owned cheese company based in Plymouth. Sargento isn't just a brand—it's a source of pride. They were one of the first companies to sell shredded cheese in resealable bags, which might not seem like a big deal, but it revolutionized the way we make tacos in Wisconsin. And for that, we're forever grateful.

Brewing Tradition: Wisconsin Beer

If there's one thing Wisconsinites love as much as cheese, it's beer. Beer is a way of life in Wisconsin, and we've got the brands to prove it. The most famous of them all is Miller, the iconic Milwaukee-based brewery that's been around since 1855. When you order a beer in Wisconsin, there's a good chance it's a Miller product—Miller Lite, Miller High Life, Miller Genuine Draft—they're all staples in the state's bar scene.

We call Miller High Life the "Champagne of Beers," and we mean it. It's the beer you drink to celebrate a big win, whether it's a Packers victory, a successful deer hunt, or the birth of your first grandchild. And if you want something a little fancier, you can go for a Spotted Cow—the flagship beer of New Glarus Brewing Company, a beloved local brand that's only available in Wisconsin. I know people who've tried to smuggle cases of Spotted Cow across state lines like it's contraband.

Leinenkugel's, based in Chippewa Falls, is another Wisconsin institution. Known for its Summer Shandy, a refreshing blend of beer and lemonade, Leinenkugel's is a go-to choice for those hot summer days when you're floating down the river or grilling brats in the backyard. They've been brewing beer since 1867, and they're not planning on stopping anytime soon.

One of the best things about Wisconsin beer brands is the way they bring people together. Whether you're at a fish fry, a tailgate, or a family reunion, beer is always part of the equation. It's a way of connecting with friends, toasting to good times, and embracing the spirit of Wisconsin hospitality.

Harleys and Hard Work: The Wisconsin Originals

There are some brands that aren't just companies—they're icons. And when it comes to Wisconsin icons, you can't beat Harley-Davidson. Founded in Milwaukee in 1903, Harley-Davidson isn't just a motorcycle manufacturer—it's a symbol of freedom, adventure, and the open road. There's something uniquely satisfying about hearing the roar of a Harley engine, knowing that it was built right here in Wisconsin.

For many Wisconsinites, owning a Harley is a lifelong dream. It's not just about the bike—it's about the culture, the community, and the pride of riding a piece of Wisconsin history. My neighbor, Gary, has been saving up for a Harley for as long as I can remember. He spends hours every weekend polishing his old, beat-up motorcycle and dreaming about the day he can upgrade to a brand-new Harley.

"I don't want just any bike, Wayne," he told me one day, wiping a tear from his eye. "I want a Harley."

Another Wisconsin original is Johnsonville, the brand that turned bratwurst into an art form. Based in Sheboygan Falls, Johnsonville is known for its high-quality sausages, which are a must-have at any brat fry or tailgate. They even have a "Bratmobile," a food truck that travels around serving up hot, juicy brats to hungry fans. And if that's not living the Wisconsin dream, I don't know what is.

Sweet Treats and Dairy Delights

No discussion of Wisconsin brands would be complete without mentioning our love of ice cream. As the Dairy State, we take our ice cream seriously, and that means supporting local brands like Culver's. Founded in Sauk City, Culver's is famous for its ButterBurgers and frozen custard. If you've never had a Culver's Concrete Mixer, you're missing out—it's like a blizzard of deliciousness, with your choice of mix-ins swirled into creamy custard.

But Culver's isn't the only game in town. There's also Babcock Hall Dairy, the University of Wisconsin-Madison's dairy store that serves up some of the best ice cream in the state. Babcock Hall's ice cream flavors are as unique as the state itself, with names like Union Utopia and Badger Blast. I've spent many a summer afternoon at Babcock Hall, indulging in a double scoop of their orange custard chocolate chip and watching the world go by.

Gear Up: Wisconsin Work Ethic

Here in Wisconsin, we know the value of hard work, and that's reflected in our brands. Take Carhartt, for example—a company that's been making durable workwear for generations of farmers, construction workers, and outdoorsmen. While not exclusive to Wisconsin, Carhartt is a staple in every Wisconsinite's closet. If you've ever shoveled snow in the dead of winter, you know that a good Carhartt jacket is worth its weight in gold.

Another Wisconsin workwear legend is Red Wing Shoes, known for their high-quality leather boots that are built to withstand the toughest conditions. Whether you're working on the farm, trekking through the woods, or just trying to survive a Wisconsin winter, Red Wing boots have got your back (or, more accurately, your feet).

A Brand for Every Occasion

One of the things I love about Wisconsin brands is that they're not just companies—they're a part of everyday life. They're the brands we turn to for comfort, celebration, and connection. Whether we're grilling Johnsonville brats, drinking Miller High Life, or cruising down the highway on a Harley, these brands remind us of where we come from and what we stand for.

And it's not just about the big names, either. It's about the small, local brands that make Wisconsin what it is. The mom-and-pop cheese shops, the family-owned bakeries, and the craft breweries that keep our traditions alive. It's about the pride we take in supporting local businesses and celebrating the things that make our state unique.

So the next time you find yourself in Wisconsin, don't just settle for the usual brands. Take a detour to Racine for a fresh kringle from O&H Danish Bakery, stop by Woodman's for a case of New Glarus beer, and pick up a bag of Copps Frozen Pizza—because if you're going to experience Wisconsin, you might as well do it right.

A Guide to Wisconsin's Best Brands

Because it's not just about cheese—it's about culture

Kwik Trip

"The Wisconsin Embassy"

If Kwik Trip were a country, its flag would be a Glazer on a pole. It's more than just a gas station—it's a gathering place for gossip, last-minute grocery runs, and existential conversations about which roller grill item will be your "meal of shame." Need a loaf of bread? A pound of butter? A hug? Kwik Trip has you covered. And don't even get us started on their rewards card—it's basically the state's second currency.

Culver's

"The Home of the ButterBurger and the Midwestern Goodbye"

Culver's is the place where you can have a burger made with butter, wash it down with a custard shake, and leave feeling like you should immediately start a diet—but won't. When you walk in, you're practically family, and by family, we mean they will always upsell you to cheese curds with a smile. Saying no is almost a sin.

Johnsonville

"For the Love of Brats"

Johnsonville is to brats what Lambeau is to football—a sacred institution. Their slogan should just be "We've Been to Every Backyard Cookout in Wisconsin." When people talk about grilling, they don't ask what kind of brats you're making—they ask *how many* Johnsonville brats you're making. The number better be in double digits.

Leinenkugel's

"For Every Occasion—Even the Ones We Just Made Up"

If you're from Wisconsin, Leinenkugel's is a requirement at every gathering. Whether it's Summer Shandy for a July fish fry or Snowdrift Vanilla Porter to pair with Aunt Nancy's infamous hotdish, Leinies has your back. Don't be surprised if someone at the bar argues that the "shandy" is a proper substitute for lemonade at a kid's birthday party—because someone definitely will.

Harley-Davidson

"Loud Pipes Save Lives and Marriages"
Harley-Davidson isn't just a motorcycle—it's a lifestyle, a cult, and a reason to wear leather chaps in July. Harley owners have a unique bond; they communicate with each other using waves, grunts, and the collective understanding that *if you haven't polished your bike at least three times this week, you're doing it wrong.* And yes, they have more Harley gear than they do socks.

Miller Brewing Company

"Official Sponsor of Family Reunions and 'Fishing Trips'"
In Wisconsin, "grabbing a Miller" doesn't just mean you're thirsty—it means you're at a wedding, a birthday party, or a Wednesday night Euchre game. Miller Lite is like water here, and Miller High Life is "the champagne of beers" because we like to keep it classy. Most Wisconsinites have a relative who insists, *"Miller invented beer, I'm telling you!"*

Sargento

"Cheese, but Fancy"
When you want to show your relatives from out of state that you're sophisticated, you serve Sargento. Their cheese is sliced so precisely that you feel compelled to arrange it on a platter like a cheese board expert—right up until your cousin Randy ruins it by stacking five slices on a single cracker and calling it a "Wisconsin Big Mac."

Land O' Lakes

"The Only Butter You Need"
If you don't have a stick of Land O' Lakes butter in your fridge, you're in danger of losing your Wisconsin citizenship. It's the kind of butter that makes you realize how much better life is with butter. Just ask the countless grandmas who swear it's the secret ingredient in every recipe from cookies to "butter soup" (which isn't a thing, but they'll make it one if you ask).

Sprecher Brewing Company

"The Root Beer of Legends"
Sprecher Root Beer is the stuff of childhood memories and adult nostalgia.

Every kid growing up in Wisconsin drinks this like it's liquid gold, and every adult remembers their first "kid hangover" after downing three bottles at a birthday party. It's a rite of passage that prepares you for the day you switch to their craft beers.

Trek Bicycles

"For When You Want to Bike Up North and Feel Smug About It"
Trek is the go-to brand for Wisconsinites who want to bike across the state or just have something to hang in their garage to make them feel athletic. Owning a Trek bike means you know the best trails, how to talk gears without sounding condescending, and that you can wear bike shorts without embarrassment—even to the Kwik Trip.

Jolly Good Soda

"It's Not a Party Without Jolly Good"
Jolly Good is the unofficial soda of Wisconsin, making appearances at every barbecue, tailgate, and late-night cheese curd run. The flavors are named things like "Sour Pow'r" and "Grape Crush," and there's no official slogan because the brand is basically fueled by pure nostalgia and a determination to outdo other states' sodas.

Blain's Farm & Fleet

"Everything You Need, Nothing You Don't"
If you need a lawnmower, work boots, and a gallon of pickles, Blain's Farm & Fleet is your one-stop shop. It's not just a store; it's an experience. You go in for windshield wiper fluid and leave with a lifetime supply of birdseed and a pair of overalls. "Impulse buys" should be renamed "Farm & Fleet finds."

Fleet Farm

"The Menard's That Also Sells Candy"
Known as "The Man Mall," Fleet Farm is where Wisconsinites go for anything from hunting gear to a new set of tires to bulk candy. It's the only place where you can buy ammo, fishing tackle, and jelly beans without anyone batting an eye. If you're from Wisconsin, you know the phrase, *"I'm just running to Fleet,"* can mean literally anything.

CHAPTER 16:
FAIRS, FESTIVALS, AND A GOOD OL' TRACTOR PULL

If there's one thing that Wisconsinites know how to do, it's throw a festival. We don't let a little thing like cold weather, sweltering heat, or the occasional rainstorm get in the way of a good time. Whether it's celebrating cheese, cranberries, fish, or polka, we find a reason to gather, eat, and enjoy life in the company of friends and strangers. Festivals in Wisconsin aren't just events—they're community traditions, passed down from one generation to the next. And if you've ever been to a county fair or witnessed the majesty of a tractor pull, you know exactly what I'm talking about.

The County Fair

The Wisconsin county fair is more than just a place to see prize-winning pigs and try your luck at a ring toss game. It's a cultural experience—a celebration of agriculture, hard work, and the simple joys of life. Every summer, families pile into their cars and head to the county fairgrounds, ready to indulge in deep-fried everything and take a spin on the Ferris wheel. It's a rite of passage, a time-honored tradition, and the highlight of summer for many Wisconsinites.

Growing up, my family never missed the Dane County Fair. We'd spend the entire day wandering through the animal barns, admiring the quilts in the craft pavilion, and sampling every deep-fried concoction we could find. My personal favorite was always the deep-fried Oreos—a decadent treat that defies both logic and dietary guidelines.

One year, my cousin Dave decided he wanted to try something new: the infamous deep-fried butter. Now, I'm not one to judge—Wisconsinites are known for our love of butter—but the idea of eating a stick of butter dipped in batter and deep-fried was enough to make my arteries tighten up in protest. Dave, however, was undeterred. He bit into it with gusto, grinning like a kid who just got away with stealing a cookie.

"Not bad," he said between bites. "Tastes like a buttery donut."

"You realize you're eating pure cholesterol, right?" I asked.

"Worth it," he replied, taking another bite.

Of course, no trip to the fair would be complete without a stop at the pig races. If you've never seen a group of pigs racing around a track, let me tell you—it's a sight to behold. The announcer calls out the pigs' names (which are usually a pun on famous athletes or celebrities), and the crowd cheers as the pigs waddle their way to the finish line. It's ridiculous, it's adorable, and it's pure Wisconsin.

But the real excitement at the fair happens after dark, when the grandstand comes alive with the roar of engines and the cheers of the crowd. I'm talking, of course, about the tractor pull—the ultimate test of power, endurance, and redneck ingenuity.

The Art of the Tractor Pull

For those of you who've never experienced a tractor pull, let me paint a picture for you. A tractor pull involves powerful tractors and modified trucks trying to pull a heavy sled as far as possible down a dirt track. It's loud, it's gritty, and it's a whole lot of fun. And in Wisconsin, tractor pulls are a big deal.

There are two types of people at a tractor pull: the people who come for the competition and the people who come for the spectacle. I'm firmly in the latter camp. I don't understand the intricacies of tractor mechanics, but I know a good show when I see one. There's something thrilling about watching a souped-up tractor kick up dirt as it roars down the track, its engine screaming like a banshee.

One summer, I took my wife to her first tractor pull. She was skeptical at first, but by the end of the night, she was hooting and hollering with the rest of us. At one point, a particularly loud tractor went by, and she turned to me with wide eyes and said, "That was awesome!"

"Welcome to the dark side," I replied, laughing.

For those who take tractor pulls seriously, it's not just about the noise and the spectacle—it's about the craftsmanship. These aren't just ordinary tractors; they're meticulously modified machines, engineered for maximum horsepower and traction. There's a certain pride that comes with building a tractor from the ground up, knowing that every bolt, every weld, and every adjustment could be the difference between victory and defeat.

My buddy Carl is a tractor pull enthusiast, and he spends all winter tinkering with his prized tractor, "The Green Monster." It's a bright green John Deere that he's modified to the point where it barely resembles a farm tractor. Every year, he enters it in the local tractor pull, hoping to take home the grand prize.

"Think you've got a shot this year?" I asked him once, admiring The Green Monster's shiny new paint job.

"Wayne," he said, grinning like a kid on Christmas morning, "this baby's got more torque than a tornado. I'm gonna blow the competition out of the water."

He didn't win that year—The Green Monster broke down halfway down the track—but that didn't dampen Carl's spirits. He spent the rest of the night celebrating with a beer in one hand and a wrench in the other, already planning his next round of modifications.

Polka, Polka, Polka

Wisconsin festivals aren't just about engines and deep-fried Oreos—they're also about music. And when it comes to music in Wisconsin, nothing gets people on their feet faster than a good polka band. Polka is a beloved part of Wisconsin's heritage, thanks to the state's strong German and Polish roots, and you can find a polka band at just about every festival, wedding, and church picnic.

One of the biggest polka festivals in the state is Polkafest in Pulaski. Every summer, polka lovers from all over Wisconsin gather in Pulaski to dance, drink, and celebrate their shared love of oompah music. The festival features live bands, dance contests, and enough pierogi to feed a small army.

Polka dancing isn't as easy as it looks. It's a workout, especially when you're trying to keep up with an 80-year-old accordion player who's got more energy than a toddler on a sugar high. But there's something infectious about polka music that makes you want to get up and dance, even if you have no idea what you're doing.

I've been to Polkafest a few times, and let me tell you—it's a blast. Even if you're not much of a dancer, it's impossible not to get caught up in the energy of the crowd. One year, I brought my friend Carl, who claimed he couldn't dance to save his life. But after a couple of beers, he was out on the dance floor, kicking up his heels like a seasoned polka pro.

"You sure you've never done this before?" I asked, grinning.

"Nope," Carl replied, breathless and smiling. "But I think I was born for this."

Cranberry Fest and Other Small-Town Celebrations

Wisconsin is home to some truly unique festivals, celebrating everything from cheese to fish to our state's most famous fruit: the cranberry. Cranberry Fest in Warrens is the largest cranberry festival in the world, drawing thousands of visitors every year. The festival features a parade, craft vendors, and, of course, plenty of cranberry-themed foods—everything from cranberry brats to cranberry pancakes.

I've been to Cranberry Fest a couple of times, and I can tell you that it's a cranberry lover's paradise. The air is filled with the scent of cranberry sauce simmering on the stove, and every booth has some new cranberry creation to try. One year, I had cranberry fudge, cranberry wine, and a cranberry-flavored cream puff—all before noon.

But what makes Cranberry Fest special isn't just the food—it's the sense of community. The whole town of Warrens gets involved, from the local farmers who grow the cranberries to the volunteers who organize the festival. It's a celebration of hard work, tradition, and the simple pleasures of small-town life.

Of course, not every festival is as well-known as Cranberry Fest. There are plenty of smaller, more obscure festivals that are just as delightful. Take the Cheese Curd Festival in Ellsworth, for example. Ellsworth is known as the "Cheese Curd Capital of Wisconsin," and every summer, they throw a festival dedicated to those squeaky little nuggets of joy. The festival features cheese curd eating contests, cheese curd cooking demonstrations, and more deep-fried cheese curds than you can shake a stick at.

And let's not forget about the Fish Boil Festival in Door County, where locals gather to watch giant kettles of fish, potatoes, and onions being boiled over an open flame. The highlight of the festival is the "boil-over," when the cook throws a handful of kerosene on the fire, causing the pot to erupt in a plume of steam and flames. It's a dramatic, delicious spectacle that never fails to impress.

The Great Wisconsin Get-Together

Of course, the biggest festival of them all is the Wisconsin State Fair. Held every August in West Allis, the State Fair is a celebration of everything that makes Wisconsin great: agriculture, food, music, and community. It's a place where you can see prize-winning cows, ride the Giant Slide, and eat your weight in cream puffs—all in the same day.

The State Fair is known for its food on a stick—corn dogs, cheese curds, chocolate-covered bacon, and even deep-fried butter. If you can eat it, you can probably find it on a stick at the State Fair. One year, I tried a deep-fried Snickers bar on a dare. It was gooey, sugary, and completely over-the-top—but surprisingly delicious.

But the real highlight of the State Fair is the cream puff. Every year, the fair sells thousands of giant cream puffs, filled with mountains of whipped cream and dusted with powdered sugar. Eating a cream puff without getting whipped cream all over yourself is an impossible task, but that's part of the fun. It's a messy, delicious tradition that every Wisconsinite embraces with pride.

I remember my first cream puff at the State Fair. I was seven years old, and my parents bought one to share. I took one bite, and the whipped cream immediately exploded out the sides, covering my face in sugary goodness. My mom tried to clean me up with a napkin, but I just grinned and licked the whipped cream off my fingers.

"Best day ever," I declared.

Community and Connection

At the end of the day, Wisconsin fairs and festivals aren't just about food, music, and tractor pulls—they're about community. They're a chance to gather with your neighbors, share a meal, and celebrate the things that make life worth living. Whether you're cheering on a friend at the tractor pull, dancing the polka with a stranger, or swapping recipes for cranberry sauce at Cranberry Fest, you're part of something bigger than yourself.

That's what makes Wisconsin special—it's not just the cheese or the beer or the festivals. It's the people, the traditions, and the sense of connection that comes from celebrating life's simple pleasures together. It's the feeling of pride you get when you bite into a deep-fried cheese curd, or when you see a little kid's face light up as they take their first spin on the Ferris wheel.

So the next time you find yourself in Wisconsin, keep an eye out for a festival or a county fair. Pull over, grab a brat or a cheese curd, and strike up a conversation with the person standing next to you. You might just make a new friend, hear a great story, or discover a new favorite food on a stick.

And if you ever get the chance to watch a tractor pull, take it—you won't regret it.

Wisconsin State Fair Tips and Tricks
For the Ultimate Dairy State Experience

1. Wear Your Comfiest Elastic Waistband Pants

Because we all know what's coming—deep-fried everything. Leave your skinny jeans at home; this is a judgment-free zone where fried cheese curds and pork chop sandwiches reign supreme.

2. Bring Cash for the Cream Puffs

The iconic Wisconsin cream puffs are practically a rite of passage, and they don't accept your excuses for not having cash. Plan to buy at least one for yourself, one to share, and one "for later" (that you'll eat before you get to your car).

3. Polish Up on Your Cheese Judging Skills

Every true Wisconsinite should be able to look at a block of cheese and determine its quality without hesitation. Practice nodding knowingly while tasting samples and saying things like, *"Oh, the aging on this cheddar is impeccable."*

4. Prep for the Weather

Bring sunscreen, a poncho, and a hoodie. It's Wisconsin in the summer, which means it could be 90 degrees, raining sideways, or dropping to 50°F by sunset. Or all three.

5. Plan a Strategy for the Animal Barns

Decide ahead of time if you're starting with the cows, sheep, or pigs. Visiting the animal barns is non-negotiable, and don't forget to congratulate at least one proud 4-H kid on their blue ribbon calf named Bessie.

6. Set a Cheese Curds Budget

Wisconsin State Fair cheese curds are not just a snack; they're a quest. Have a budget in mind and know your cheese curd stands by name. When someone asks, *"Where'd you get those curds?"* you should be ready with specific directions and a Yelp-worthy review.

7. Wear Comfortable Shoes (Not Sandals!)

You're going to be on your feet all day, and the fairgrounds are huge. Flip-flops might sound appealing, but the number of stepping-on incidents increases with every brat and lemonade you consume.

8. Map Out Your Deep-Fried Itinerary

The Wisconsin State Fair is a showcase of culinary creativity (or madness). From deep-fried Oreos to chocolate-covered bacon, have a game plan to hit all the must-try stands. Just don't overdo it with the deep-fried pickles—you've been warned.

9. Get Your "Packer Polka" Dance Moves Ready

There will be at least one local band playing a polka version of the Packers fight song. Practice your dance moves so you can look like a pro (or at least avoid injuring the people dancing next to you).

10. Take the Giant Slide Challenge

If you're going to the Wisconsin State Fair, the Giant Slide is a must. Embrace the 15 seconds of sheer thrill and bragging rights, and try not to scream like a kid. Bonus points if you race a friend down!

11. Prepare for "Friendly" Livestock Competitions

The cow judging can get heated. Be prepared for polite but intense debates about which cow has the best coat and why Bessie the Third was robbed of first place.

12. Plan Your Evening Around the Pig Races

You don't leave the Wisconsin State Fair without watching at least one pig race. Choose a pig to cheer for, give it a name like "Hammy Rodgers," and scream like your pig's running for the Lombardi Trophy.

13. Schedule a Corn Dog Break

It's not a real fair experience without eating a corn dog (or five). Have a designated corn dog time so you don't miss your chance—plus, it's the perfect mid-day snack while you rest your feet.

14. Drink a Bloody Mary the Size of Your Head

Some of the fair's Bloody Marys come with more garnishes than a Thanksgiving dinner. Be prepared to tackle a drink that includes skewers of cheese, sausage, olives, a pickle spear, and possibly an entire chicken wing.

15. Take a Break at the Real Wisconsin Cheese Pavilion

If all the fried food is getting to you, head to the Real Wisconsin Cheese Pavilion for samples. It's a safe space where you can consume cheese guilt-free and nod knowingly while listening to cheesemakers discuss curd squeak levels.

16. Play "Count the FIBs"

You'll spot Illinois visitors, aka FIBs ("Friendly Illinois Buddies"), a mile away. Make a game of counting their Bears shirts and Cubs hats. Bonus points if you overhear a FIB ordering a beer and saying *"go packers"* just to fit in.

17. Don't Miss the Butter Cow

Every Wisconsinite knows the Butter Cow is the Mona Lisa of the fair. Take a picture, contemplate its beauty, and then argue with your friends about what kind of toast you'd spread it on.

18. Hit the Midway, But Know Your Limits

The Midway is where you can relive your youth by playing games you're sure you can win (you won't) and going on rides that remind you why you took that Tums earlier. Know when to call it a day—or at least when to avoid the Tilt-a-Whirl after eating three corn dogs.

19. Bring a Reusable Bag for the Freebies

You'll collect brochures, keychains, and promotional yardsticks from every booth you pass. Be prepared with a bag so you can carry your loot without losing your hand-dipped corn-on-the-cob.

20. End the Night with a Funnel Cake

There's only one way to end your State Fair experience: with a funnel cake dusted in enough powdered sugar to make you look like you've aged 50 years. It's the perfect way to cap off a day of cheese, rides, and Wisconsin pride.

CHAPTER 17:
ICE FISHING AND OTHER FROZEN ADVENTURES

When most people think of winter in Wisconsin, they think of snow, ice, and temperatures so cold they make your face hurt. But here in the Dairy State, we don't let a little thing like freezing temperatures keep us indoors. In fact, we embrace the cold, and we find ways to turn winter into an adventure. One of the most iconic Wisconsin winter traditions is ice fishing—a pastime that combines the joy of fishing with the thrill of sitting on a frozen lake for hours on end.

Ice fishing isn't just a hobby in Wisconsin—it's a way of life. It's an opportunity to escape the house, breathe in the crisp winter air, and bond with friends over the shared experience of freezing your tail off. And while it might sound crazy to outsiders, to us, it's just another way to enjoy the beauty of a Wisconsin winter.

The Ice Fishing Shanty

Every winter, as soon as the ice is thick enough to walk on, the lakes of Wisconsin become dotted with ice fishing shanties. These small, makeshift huts are like tiny homes on the ice, offering a (somewhat) warm refuge from the cold winds. Inside, you'll find everything you need for a day of fishing: a folding chair, a space heater, a cooler of beer, and maybe even a small TV hooked up to a car battery.

My buddy Carl has a shanty that he's been using for years. It's nothing fancy—just a wooden box with a small stove and a couple of holes drilled in the ice—but it's cozy in its own way. Carl calls it "The Fish Palace," and he takes great pride in decorating it with Packers posters and a collection of old beer signs.

One winter, Carl invited me out for a day of ice fishing on Lake Mendota. When I arrived at the lake, he was already inside the shanty, sipping a beer and listening to the Packers pre-game show on the radio.

"Welcome to The Fish Palace," he said, gesturing to the folding chair next to him. "Make yourself at home."

I sat down and looked around. The walls were covered in pictures of past ice fishing trips, and there was a small shelf stocked with fishing gear, snacks, and a collection of mismatched coffee mugs. The whole place smelled like a combination of fish, beer, and wood smoke—a surprisingly comforting scent.

"This is nice," I said, taking a sip of my coffee.

"Yep," Carl replied, leaning back in his chair. "Nothing like spending a day on the ice."

The Art of Catching Nothing

If there's one thing I've learned about ice fishing, it's that catching fish isn't really the point. Sure, it's nice to reel in a big walleye or a few panfish, but for most ice fishermen, the real joy comes from simply being out on the ice, away from the hustle and bustle of everyday life. It's a chance to slow down, enjoy the quiet, and maybe even reflect on the mysteries of the universe—or at least the mysteries of why fish aren't biting.

On that particular day, Carl and I spent hours staring at our fishing lines, waiting for a nibble. The wind howled outside, and the temperature inside the shanty hovered just above freezing. Every now and then, Carl would take a sip of his beer, adjust his line, and mutter, "Any day now."

After a while, I decided to ask the obvious question. "Do you actually catch fish out here?" I asked.

Carl chuckled. "Sometimes," he said. "But not today, apparently."

We sat in silence for a few more minutes, and then Carl turned to me with a grin. "You know what my grandpa used to say?" he asked.

"What's that?" I replied.

"He used to say, 'Ice fishing isn't about catching fish—it's about not being at home,'" Carl said, laughing. "And the older I get, the more I understand what he meant."

The Great Ice Fishing Cookout

One of the best parts of ice fishing is the cookout. After a few hours on the ice, nothing hits the spot like a hot brat or a bowl of chili. It's a tradition among Wisconsin ice fishermen to bring a portable grill or a small propane stove, so you can cook up a hearty meal without ever leaving the lake.

Carl, of course, takes his ice fishing cookouts very seriously. He's got a portable grill that he sets up outside the shanty, along with a folding table and a cooler full of brats, burgers, and venison steaks. One winter, he even brought a cast-iron skillet and made a batch of his famous "Shanty Stew"—a concoction of ground beef, potatoes, onions, and whatever else he could find in his freezer.

"Secret ingredient?" I asked, as I watched him stir the stew.

"Leftover venison sausage," Carl replied, grinning. "Gives it a little extra kick."

As the stew simmered on the grill, we gathered around, huddling close to the warmth of the fire. The sun was starting to set, casting a golden glow over the ice, and the air was filled with the smell of grilled meat and wood smoke. It was a perfect moment, the kind that makes you forget about the cold and the long winter ahead.

"You know," Carl said, taking a sip of his beer, "there's something magical about being out here. It's like the rest of the world just fades away."

I nodded in agreement. He was right. There's a certain serenity that comes with ice fishing—a sense of peace that's hard to find anywhere else.

Ice Fishing Legends and Tall Tales

Like any good Wisconsin tradition, ice fishing comes with its fair share of tall tales. Every ice fisherman has a story about the "one that got away" or the time they caught a fish so big it barely fit through the hole in the ice. And while some of these stories are undoubtedly exaggerated, that doesn't make them any less entertaining.

One winter, Carl and I were out on the ice with a group of friends, swapping fishing stories around the grill. Old man Jenkins, who's been ice fishing for longer than I've been alive, started telling us about the time he caught a "legendary walleye" that weighed at least 20 pounds.

"I was out here all by myself," Jenkins began, leaning forward for dramatic effect. "It was a quiet day—no wind, no snow, just me and the lake. And all of a sudden, my line goes taut, and I know I've got something big on the other end."

He paused, taking a sip of his coffee. "I fought that fish for what felt like hours," he continued. "It pulled, I pulled, back and forth, back and forth. And finally, I got it up to the hole, and let me tell you—this walleye was a monster. Must've been at least three feet long, with teeth like a bear trap."

"What happened next?" I asked, genuinely curious.

Jenkins sighed, shaking his head. "Just as I was about to pull it through the hole, the line snapped," he said. "That walleye swam off, and I never saw it again."

We all nodded solemnly, as if paying our respects to the lost fish. And while I had my doubts about the size of Jenkins' "legendary walleye," I wasn't about to question his story. After all, in Wisconsin, fishing tales are a matter of tradition—and a little embellishment never hurt anyone.

The Polar Plunge

Ice fishing isn't the only winter adventure Wisconsinites enjoy. There's also the Polar Plunge—a tradition that involves jumping into an icy lake to raise money for charity. It's a combination of bravery, foolishness, and community spirit, and it's one of the most exhilarating ways to embrace the cold.

One year, my wife convinced me to participate in the Polar Plunge. I was hesitant at first—I'm not exactly a fan of jumping into freezing water—but she assured me it would be fun.

"Come on, Wayne," she said, grinning. "It's for a good cause."

I reluctantly agreed, and before I knew it, we were standing on the edge of a hole in the ice, wearing matching T-shirts that read "Team Larson." The crowd cheered as the announcer called out our names, and my heart started pounding as I looked down at the dark, icy water below.

"You ready?" my wife asked, taking my hand.

"Not even a little bit," I replied, laughing nervously.

But there was no turning back. We counted to three, took a deep breath, and jumped.

The shock of the cold water hit me like a freight train. It felt like a thousand needles stabbing my skin, and for a moment, I couldn't breathe. But then, as quickly as it came, the shock faded, and I felt a strange rush of exhilaration. We scrambled out of the water, laughing and shivering, and wrapped ourselves in warm towels.

"That was insane," I said, grinning from ear to ear.

"Yep," my wife replied, smiling. "Let's do it again next year."

Embracing the Cold

For many people, the idea of spending hours on a frozen lake or jumping into an icy river sounds like pure madness. But for Wisconsinites, it's just another way to embrace the cold and make the most of winter. It's about finding joy in the little things, whether it's the warmth of a shanty stove, the thrill of a big catch, or the laughter of friends gathered around a grill.

And while winter in Wisconsin can be harsh, it's also beautiful. There's something magical about the way the snow sparkles in the moonlight, or the way the ice on the lake cracks and groans like it's alive. It's a reminder that even in the coldest, darkest months, there's still warmth to be found—in the company of friends, in the comfort of a hot meal, and in the simple pleasure of a day well spent on the ice.

A Tradition Worth Keeping

In the end, ice fishing and other winter adventures aren't just about braving the cold—they're about celebrating life in the Great White North. They're a chance to connect with nature, spend time with friends, and create memories that will last a lifetime. And in a state where winters can be long and unforgiving, those memories are worth their weight in gold.

So the next time you find yourself in Wisconsin during the winter, don't be afraid to embrace the cold. Grab your fishing gear, find a spot on the ice, and take a deep breath of that crisp winter air. And if you're lucky, you might just catch a glimpse of the legendary walleye—or at the very least, a story worth telling.

And if someone invites you to take a Polar Plunge, just remember: it's all for a good cause.

The Polar Plunge: A Midwestern Rite

In Wisconsin land where winters bite,
Where lakes freeze solid every night,
Comes a challenge brave folks arrange—
The annual Polar Plunge exchange.

Bundled up in hats and coats,
We gather 'round with nervous throats.
"Why are we doing this?" whispers Jane,
Who's lost three toes to frostbite pain.

The lake looks like a giant slushy—
Murky, cold, and quite untrusty.
"I'll go first!" shouts cousin Hank,
Who downed two brandies to build his plank.

The crowd cheers, full of thrill,
As Hank disrobes on the icy hill.
He's down to shorts—oh, what a sight!
Socks with sandals, legs ghostly white.

With a whoop and a holler, he charges in,
Doing his best to fight the wind.
But when that icy water hits,
His face contorts, and he loses his wits.

"Holy cripes, it's freezing!" he yells aloud,
Echoing back through the shivering crowd.
His body reacts like he's doing the worm,
As he tries to retreat with grace and firm.

Next up is Brenda, she's not one to stall—
"Let's get this over with," she yells to all.
She dives in headfirst, like she's on TV,
Emerging with goosebumps the size of a pea.

"Why did I do this? What's wrong with my brain?"
She sputters and shivers but laughs through the pain.
The crowd claps politely, their turn drawing near,
Each wondering why they signed up this year.

Bob's false teeth clatter as he heads to the edge,
Marge in her flannel is making a pledge:
"If I don't survive this, tell my kids,
That their mother went out with frost on her lids."

The plunge continues, one by one,
They scream, they jump, they cry "Well, that's done!"
Out of the lake, wrapped in towels they waddle,
Straight to the bonfire to "get warm with a toddle."

When it's all over, and everyone's thawed,
They brag and they boast, and they applaud.
"Wasn't so bad!" they all agree,
Though their feet look like they've just crossed the sea.

But as the chill leaves their bones, one thing remains,
The annual honor, the Midwestern gains—
To say they plunged where the brave never budge,
And to earn their hot cocoa with an extra fudge.

So next year when the snowbanks pile high,
And folks are looking for new ways to die,
They'll head to the lake with bravado so strange,
And once again, take that Polar Plunge exchange.

CHAPTER 18:
FRIDAY NIGHT LIGHTS AND FISH FRY DELIGHTS

Friday night in Wisconsin is a sacred time. For most places in the country, Friday night might mean hitting up a trendy restaurant, catching a movie, or collapsing on the couch with takeout. But here in Wisconsin, it means two things: high school football and Friday night fish fry. And sometimes, if you're lucky, those two traditions combine to create the perfect Wisconsin evening.

The Friday night fish fry is more than just a meal—it's a celebration of community, tradition, and the end of another long workweek. It's a time to gather with friends and family, swap stories, and enjoy a plate of crispy, golden-brown fish with all the fixings. And while the fish fry might seem simple to outsiders, to Wisconsinites, it's a time-honored ritual that's as comforting as a warm blanket on a cold night.

The High School Football Frenzy

In small towns across Wisconsin, Friday night means high school football. The local stadiums fill up with parents, students, and alumni, all eager to cheer on their hometown team. The air is thick with the smell of popcorn, the sound of marching bands, and the excitement of a community coming together.

Growing up, my family never missed a game. My dad was a die-hard fan of our high school's team, the Pineville Panthers, and he always made sure we were in the stands, rain or shine. He'd bring a thermos of hot chocolate for the cold games, and a portable fan for the sweltering ones. And he had a special way of showing his support: a foam finger with the words "Go Panthers!" written on it in glitter glue (courtesy of my mom's arts and crafts skills).

Every game was a spectacle. The cheerleaders did their routines, the marching band played the fight song, and the fans cheered like their lives depended on it. And while the game itself was the main event, there was always a sense of camaraderie in the stands—a feeling that we were all part of something bigger than ourselves.

One Friday night, when I was in high school, our team was down by a touchdown in the final minutes of the game. The tension in the stands was palpable, and everyone was on the edge of their seats. My dad, who usually stayed pretty calm during games, was gripping his foam finger so tightly I thought it might snap in half.

"Come on, Panthers," he muttered, almost like a prayer.

And then, in a moment that still gives me goosebumps, our quarterback threw a Hail Mary pass that sailed through the air and landed perfectly in the hands of our star receiver. The crowd went wild, the marching band started playing, and my dad jumped up and down like a kid on Christmas morning.

"That's what I'm talking about!" he yelled, waving his foam finger triumphantly.

It was a night I'll never forget, and it taught me an important lesson: in Wisconsin, high school football is more than just a game—it's a way of life.

The Fish Fry Feast

After the game, there's only one place to go: the local supper club for a Friday night fish fry. In Wisconsin, the fish fry is a weekly tradition, a ritual that brings people together to share a meal and unwind after a long week. And while every supper club has its own unique twist on the fish fry, the essentials are always the same: crispy fried fish, coleslaw, rye bread, and a cold beer.

My family's go-to spot was The Pine Tree Lodge, a classic supper club with wood-paneled walls, taxidermy on the walls, and a bartender who knew everyone by name. The place was always packed on Friday nights, and there was usually a line out the door. But no one minded the wait—half the fun of a fish fry is standing at the bar, chatting with friends and sipping on a brandy Old Fashioned.

My dad's order was always the same: "All-you-can-eat perch, potato pancakes, and extra tartar sauce." He liked to joke that he could eat his weight in perch, and I'm pretty sure he wasn't exaggerating. My mom, on the other hand, was a fan of the walleye, which she claimed was the "classy" choice. And as for me, I was happy with a plate of beer-battered cod and a side of French fries.

One Friday night, after a particularly exciting football game, we headed to The Pine Tree Lodge for our usual post-game fish fry. The place was buzzing with energy, and it seemed like half the town was there, still wearing their team colors and talking about the big win.

We found a table near the back, and as we waited for our food, we chatted with some of the other regulars. There was old man Jenkins, who always had a fishing story to share, and my dad's friend Carl, who insisted that the key to a perfect fish fry was "all about the batter." There was even a table of cheerleaders celebrating the victory, still wearing their uniforms and laughing like they didn't have a care in the world.

When our food arrived, it was a feast fit for a king. The fish was perfectly golden and crispy, the coleslaw was tangy and refreshing, and the potato pancakes were just the right amount of greasy. My dad took one bite of his perch, nodded in approval, and said, "Now that's what I'm talking about."

The Great Fish Fry Debate

Like any good Wisconsin tradition, the Friday night fish fry comes with its share of debates. Some people swear by perch, while others insist that cod is the only way to go. There's the age-old argument about potato pancakes versus French fries, and let's not even get started on the topic of tartar sauce.

My dad and his buddy Jim had an ongoing debate about the best fish fry in town. My dad was a loyal fan of The Pine Tree Lodge, while Jim swore by Al's Lakeview, a supper club with a killer view of the lake and a fish fry that Jim claimed was "to die for."

"Al's Lakeview has the best potato pancakes in the state," Jim said one night, taking a sip of his Old Fashioned.

"Oh, please," my dad replied, rolling his eyes. "The Pine Tree Lodge's potato pancakes are crispy on the outside, fluffy on the inside, and not too greasy. They're perfection."

"Yeah, but Al's has the best tartar sauce," Jim countered. "It's got just the right amount of tang."

"Who cares about the tartar sauce?" my dad shot back. "It's all about the fish."

This back-and-forth went on for years, with no clear winner. In the end, they usually agreed to disagree and ordered another round of Old Fashioneds. After all, in Wisconsin, it's not just about the food—it's about the camaraderie and the shared experience of a good fish fry.

The Supper Club Etiquette

There's a certain etiquette to dining at a Wisconsin supper club, and it's something every local learns instinctively. For starters, you should always arrive early and have a drink at the bar while you wait for your table. It's not just about passing the time—it's about soaking in the atmosphere and catching up with friends.

When you're at the bar, it's customary to order a brandy Old Fashioned, sweet with 7-Up. If you ask for a beer, that's fine, but you might get a few raised eyebrows. And if you dare to order a martini, the bartender might suggest you try the steak instead.

Once you're seated, it's time to order your fish. And here's where the etiquette really comes into play: if it's your first time at a particular supper club, it's polite to ask the waiter for a recommendation. Locals know that every supper club has its specialty, whether it's the beer-battered walleye, the perch with lemon butter, or the bluegill that's been fried to perfection.

And don't forget to order a side of potato pancakes—they're a must-have. Just be sure to leave room for dessert, because no supper club experience is complete without a grasshopper, that minty ice cream drink that's the perfect way to end a meal.

A Night to Remember

For me, the combination of high school football and Friday night fish fry is the ultimate expression of Wisconsin culture. It's a celebration of community, tradition, and the simple pleasures of life. It's about cheering for your team, sharing a meal with friends, and embracing the things that make Wisconsin special.

One Friday night, after a particularly thrilling football game and a hearty fish fry, I remember sitting at the table with my family, feeling a deep sense of contentment. The game had been a nail-biter, the fish fry had been delicious, and the company had been even better.

As we finished our meal, my dad raised his glass and said, "Here's to Friday nights—may they always be full of football and fish."

We all clinked our glasses, and in that moment, I realized that Friday nights in Wisconsin weren't just about the game or the food—they were about the memories we were creating, the traditions we were passing down, and the sense of belonging that comes from being part of a community.

So the next time you find yourself in Wisconsin on a Friday night, do yourself a favor: head to the local high school stadium, cheer for the home team, and then make your way to the nearest supper club for a fish fry. Order the perch, try the potato pancakes, and don't forget to save room for dessert. Because in Wisconsin, there's no better way to spend a Friday night.

The Ultimate Guide to Planning for a Friday Night in Wisconsin

Because in the Dairy State, Friday isn't just a day—it's a lifestyle

Step 1: Confirm the Friday Night Fish Fry Plans

It's Friday, which means you're going to a fish fry. It's not a question of if, but where. Start by messaging your group chat, "Fish fry tonight?" and wait for a chorus of "You betcha!" to roll in. Call ahead to your local supper club or bar and grill to avoid waiting an hour while awkwardly watching the people already eating.

Step 2: Secure the Proper Attire

Dress code is "Wisconsin Casual," which means jeans, a Packers hoodie, and boots sturdy enough to handle snow, mud, or spilled beer. Leave your fancy shoes at home and grab that Packers beanie your grandma knitted you—it'll get you a few extra "Nice hat!" compliments at the bar.

Step 3: Do a Kwik Trip Run

You're going to need supplies: a 6-pack of Spotted Cow, some Glazers for the morning (or for the ride home if you're feeling wild), and maybe a pre-fish fry snack. Kwik Trip is the one-stop shop for anything you might have forgotten or suddenly realized you desperately need. Also, don't forget to fill up on gas while you're there—it's basically tradition.

Step 4: Organize the Fish Fry Convoy

Coordinate the carpool to the fish fry spot. Every group needs at least one designated driver, one person to play DJ, and one friend who talks too loudly about the Packers' chances this season. Pro tip: make sure you have room in the back for to-go boxes. There will be leftovers.

Step 5: Prepare for Fish Fry Etiquette

Once you arrive, do a polite "Ope, sorry!" as you squeeze through the crowd. Find your table, order a round of Old Fashioneds (brandy sweet, of course), and make small talk about how the weather's been lately. When the fish arrives, discuss the merits of cod versus perch in great detail, as if you're on a cooking show.

Step 6: Hit Up the Local Watering Hole

After the fish fry, it's time to head to your favorite local dive bar. This is where the real fun begins. Pick a bar with pool tables, dartboards, and a jukebox loaded with polka hits and '80s rock. Order a round of drinks for the table, and be prepared to wave at literally everyone who walks in, even if you don't know them. It's Wisconsin—everyone waves.

Step 7: Engage in Competitive Bar Games

Choose your sport—darts, pool, or shuffleboard. Inevitably, someone in your group will be a self-proclaimed expert at one of these, and you'll all have to listen to them explain "proper form" while you're just trying to have a good time. Remember, the goal is not to win but to trash-talk your friends and laugh about it.

Step 8: Order a Late-Night Pizza

It's almost midnight, and you need something to soak up all those Old Fashioneds and Spotted Cows. Call the local pizza joint (the one that's been there since the '80s and makes their sauce from scratch) and order a large, extra cheesy pie. If you're really feeling ambitious, throw in some cheese breadsticks and extra marinara.

Step 9: Plan the Next Morning's Recovery Strategy

Before heading home, do a quick inventory of your supplies: water bottles, ibuprofen, and a solid breakfast plan for tomorrow. A Kwik Trip breakfast sandwich is always a safe bet, but if you're lucky, someone might be planning to make pancakes. Arrange to meet for brunch, where you'll recap the night's adventures and plan next week's fish fry.

Step 10: End the Night with a Wisconsin Goodbye

The Wisconsin Goodbye isn't just a wave—it's a series of mini-conversations by the car, a "Thanks for coming out!", and another five-minute discussion about the weather. Then, one final "Ope, take care now!" before you actually leave.

Bonus Tips for an Epic Friday Night:

- Remember Your Polka Moves: You never know when a polka song might come on, and you'll need to be ready.

- Have Some Packers Trivia Up Your Sleeve: It'll come in handy at the bar.

- Bring Extra Cash for the Jukebox: You don't want to be the one who's stuck listening to a five-song country playlist.

- Practice Your Cheese Curds Review: You'll inevitably be asked which place has the best, and you need to sound like a pro.

CHAPTER 19:
THE GREAT OUTDOORS: CAMPING, CANOEING, AND CAMPFIRE STORIES

When summer finally arrives in Wisconsin, we all breathe a collective sigh of relief. The snow has melted, the lakes have thawed, and the scent of fresh-cut grass fills the air. And while summer might be short, Wisconsinites know how to make the most of it. For many of us, that means packing up the car, grabbing a cooler full of brats and beer, and heading out into the great outdoors.

Whether it's a weekend camping trip, a day of canoeing on the river, or an evening spent swapping stories around the campfire, there's something about being outside in the Wisconsin wilderness that just feels right. It's a chance to unplug, reconnect with nature, and create memories that last a lifetime. And in a state that's home to more than 15,000 lakes, endless forests, and some of the friendliest mosquitoes you'll ever meet, there's no shortage of adventures to be had.

The Camping Tradition

Camping is a Wisconsin rite of passage, a tradition that's been passed down from one generation to the next. And while every family has its own way of doing things, the essentials are always the same: a tent, a campfire, and a cooler full of snacks. Some folks like to rough it in the wilderness, while others prefer the comforts of an RV with all the modern amenities. But no matter how you choose to camp, the goal is the same: to get away from it all and enjoy the simple pleasures of life.

My family's favorite camping spot was Devil's Lake State Park, a stunning park with hiking trails, towering bluffs, and a crystal-clear lake that's perfect for swimming and fishing. Every summer, we'd spend a weekend at Devil's Lake, pitching our tents in the same spot and setting up our campsite like it was our second home.

My dad was the campfire master, and he took his role very seriously. He'd spend hours gathering kindling, arranging the logs just so, and meticulously tending to the fire until it was burning bright and strong. And once the fire was roaring, it was time for the best part of camping: s'mores.

"Gotta get the marshmallow just right," my dad would say, holding his marshmallow over the flames. "Golden brown on the outside, gooey on the inside."

My mom, on the other hand, was in charge of the campfire stories. She had a talent for spinning tall tales that left us both laughing and looking over our shoulders. One of her favorites was the story of Old Man Wenzel, a legendary figure who was said to roam the woods at night, searching for campers who dared to steal his firewood.

"Don't leave your fire unattended," she'd warn, her voice dropping to a whisper. "Or Old Man Wenzel might pay you a visit."

We knew it was all in good fun, but that didn't stop us from glancing nervously at the dark woods beyond the campfire.

Canoeing on the Wisconsin River

For many Wisconsinites, summer wouldn't be complete without a canoeing trip down one of the state's many rivers. The Wisconsin River is a popular choice, with its calm waters, scenic sandbars, and occasional wildlife sightings. Canoeing is a chance to escape the hustle and bustle of everyday life, trade the sound of traffic for the call of loons, and maybe even catch a glimpse of an eagle soaring overhead.

One summer, my buddy Carl convinced me to join him on a weekend canoe trip down the Wisconsin River. Carl, who prides himself on being a "rugged outdoorsman," insisted that it would be a relaxing, leisurely trip.

"It's just you, me, and the river," he said, grinning. "What could go wrong?"

As it turned out, a lot could go wrong. We underestimated the strength of the current, overestimated our paddling skills, and managed to tip the canoe not once, but twice. By the end of the first day, we were soaked, sunburned, and questioning our life choices.

But despite the mishaps, there was something undeniably peaceful about drifting down the river, the sun setting behind the trees and the water reflecting the sky's changing colors. We spent the evenings camping on sandy riverbanks, grilling brats over a portable grill, and laughing about our less-than-stellar canoeing skills.

On the last night of the trip, as we sat around the campfire, Carl raised his beer and said, "Here's to surviving another adventure."

I clinked my can against his. "Barely," I replied, smiling.

Fishing, Fires, and Friendly Critters

If there's one thing every Wisconsin camper knows, it's that you're never truly alone in the woods. From the curious raccoons that raid your cooler to the relentless mosquitoes that see you as an all-you-can-eat buffet, camping in Wisconsin comes with its fair share of critter encounters.

One summer, while camping at Mirror Lake State Park, my family had an unexpected visitor: a particularly bold raccoon that we dubbed "Rocky." Rocky showed up on the first night, rifling through our garbage and making off with a bag of marshmallows. My dad chased him off with a broom, muttering something about "those pesky raccoons," but Rocky wasn't deterred.

The next morning, we woke up to find that Rocky had returned during the night and managed to pry the lid off our cooler. He'd made off with a pack of hot dogs and a loaf of bread, leaving behind a trail of paw prints and a sense of admiration for his persistence.

"He's a crafty one," my dad admitted, shaking his head.

But not all critter encounters are as amusing. There's nothing quite like the sound of a buzzing mosquito in your tent at two in the morning, or the discovery of a spider the size of a quarter crawling across your sleeping bag. These little annoyances are just part of the camping experience, and over time, you learn to take them in stride.

One trick I learned from my dad is to hang a campsite citronella lantern to keep the mosquitoes at bay. He swore by it, claiming that it was the only thing standing between us and a swarm of bloodthirsty insects. And while I was skeptical at first, I have to admit—it worked like a charm.

The Magic of the Night Sky

One of the things I love most about camping in Wisconsin is the chance to see the night sky in all its glory. Far away from the city lights, the stars shine brighter, the constellations are clearer, and the Milky Way stretches across the sky like a shimmering river. It's a sight that never fails to leave me in awe, no matter how many times I see it.

One summer, while camping at Peninsula State Park, my wife and I stayed up late to watch a meteor shower. We spread out a blanket on the grass, lay back, and stared up at the sky, counting shooting stars and making wishes on each one.

"Do you ever feel small when you look at the stars?" my wife asked, her voice barely more than a whisper.

"Sometimes," I replied. "But mostly, I just feel lucky to be here."

It was one of those moments that makes you appreciate the beauty of the world and the simple joy of being outside, surrounded by the people you love.

A Tradition Worth Keeping

For many Wisconsinites, spending time in the great outdoors isn't just a pastime—it's a tradition that's deeply ingrained in our culture. It's about passing down the skills and stories of previous generations, teaching your kids how to bait a hook, and creating memories that will last long after the campfire has burned out.

One summer, my dad decided it was time to teach me how to start a campfire. He showed me how to gather kindling, build a teepee of logs, and use a single match to get the fire going. I was nervous at first, but with his guidance, I managed to get the fire started.

"Good job, Wayne," he said, patting me on the back. "You're a real outdoorsman now."

It was a small moment, but it meant the world to me. It was a reminder that the traditions we pass down—no matter how simple—are a way of connecting with the past, honoring the present, and preparing for the future.

A Place to Unwind and Unplug

In a world that's always moving, always connected, and always demanding our attention, there's something incredibly refreshing about unplugging and spending a few days in the great outdoors. It's a chance to slow down, breathe deeply, and appreciate the beauty of the world around us. It's about trading the noise of the city for the sound of birdsong, the glow of a screen for the glow of a campfire, and the rush of everyday life for the quiet rhythm of the woods.

So the next time you find yourself in Wisconsin, take a break from the hustle and bustle, pack up your camping gear, and head out into the wilderness. Find a quiet spot by the lake, set up your tent, and build a campfire that crackles and dances in the night. Roast a marshmallow, tell a tall tale, and take a moment to look up at the stars.

Because in Wisconsin, the great outdoors isn't just a place to visit—it's a place to belong.

Ultimate Wisconsin Camping Checklist

For a Weekend in the Great Outdoors (and Maybe a Few "Ope!" Moments)

Essentials

- [ ] **Tent**: Make sure it's waterproof (this isn't your backyard sleepover).
- [ ] **Sleeping Bag**: Rated for 20°F below what you expect—Wisconsin weather is sneaky.
- [ ] **Camping Chairs**: You'll need these for sitting around the campfire and making small talk about who's snoring the loudest.
- [ ] **Cooler**: Preferably large enough to fit a week's worth of beer and brats.
- [ ] **Firewood**: Don't assume there'll be a pile of logs waiting for you. Bring some, and save yourself the shame of begging from your neighbors.

Cooking Gear

- [ ] **Portable Grill or Camp Stove**: Because a campfire can only do so much when you're trying to make pancakes.
- [ ] **Cast Iron Skillet**: It's a rite of passage to accidentally burn something in this.
- [ ] **Dutch Oven**: If you're feeling fancy and want to bake a cobbler or a hotdish.
- [ ] **Tongs and Spatula**: For flipping brats and pancakes, respectively (don't mix those up).
- [ ] **Utensils, Plates, and Mugs**: Preferably the ones with little fish or deer designs that say *"I'm a serious camper."*

Food and Drinks

- [ ] **Brats, Cheese, and Beer**: The holy trinity of Wisconsin camping cuisine.
- [ ] **Coffee**: Enough to keep you functional after sleeping on the ground. Bring a percolator if you want to impress.
- [ ] **S'mores Supplies**: Graham crackers, marshmallows, and chocolate—the staples of every successful camping trip.
- [ ] **Snacks**: Cheese curds (they don't need refrigeration, right?), beef jerky, and trail mix that's mostly chocolate.

☐ **Breakfast Essentials**: Eggs, bacon, and pancake mix. Don't forget the maple syrup—preferably the real stuff from Up North.

Clothing and Footwear

☐ **Layered Clothing**: Plan for all four seasons—often in the same day.
☐ **Rain Jacket**: Not for *if*, but *when* the rain comes.
☐ **Warm Socks**: Double up if your feet get cold easily (or if you don't trust your tent-mate's toe-warming skills).
☐ **Hiking Boots**: Sturdy enough for trails, muddy enough to prove you used them.
☐ **Hat and Sunglasses**: To protect you from the sun and to complete the *"I'm a seasoned outdoorsman"* look.

Campfire Supplies

☐ **Matches or Lighter**: Bring extras, because losing them is practically tradition.
☐ **Fire Starters**: Dry tinder, newspaper, or a buddy with old love letters he's ready to burn.
☐ **Marshmallow Roasting Sticks**: Long enough to keep your fingers intact while reaching over the flames.

Comfort and Safety Gear

☐ **Bug Spray**: Enough to share with the entire campsite, and then some.
☐ **Sunscreen**: SPF 50, because Wisconsin sunburns are no joke.
☐ **First Aid Kit**: For minor cuts, scrapes, and when Uncle Carl slices his finger trying to open a can.
☐ **Flashlights and Headlamps**: Don't forget extra batteries! You'll need them for midnight bathroom trips and when you *think* you hear a bear.
☐ **Swiss Army Knife or Multi-Tool**: For cutting rope, opening bottles, and impressing your friends with your "preparedness."

Fun and Activities

☐ **Fishing Gear**: Rods, reels, tackle box, and a good fish story you can retell for the hundredth time.
☐ **Board Games and Cards**: For when it rains or when someone

claims they're "the Euchre champion."

- [ ] **Books or Nature Guides**: For pretending you're going to read them while actually staring into the campfire.
- [ ] **Camera or Binoculars**: For wildlife spotting, star-gazing, or proving you were *Up North* without having to talk about it.

Personal Items

- [ ] **Toiletries**: Toothbrush, toothpaste, soap, deodorant (for the benefit of everyone).
- [ ] **Toilet Paper**: Don't rely on the campground bathrooms being stocked. Bring your own TP or face the consequences.
- [ ] **Towel**: For swimming, drying off, and maybe wiping away tears when you realize you forgot half your stuff.

Miscellaneous Must-Haves

- [ ] **Duct Tape**: For tent repairs, bandaging egos, and basically everything.
- [ ] **Rope or Paracord**: For clotheslines, bear bags, and making your campsite look extra official.
- [ ] **Hammock**: Because it's not camping if you don't nap under the trees.
- [ ] **Trash Bags**: Leave no trace behind, except maybe some half-burned marshmallows.
- [ ] **Camping Spirit**: Don't forget to bring a good attitude, a sense of humor, and a willingness to over-exaggerate how rough the weekend was when you tell the story later.

Pro Tip:

If you get cold or your tent leaks, remember to blame it on the *"dang unpredictable Wisconsin weather"* and not on the fact that you bought a cheap tent from Fleet Farm. And when you get home, don't forget to tell everyone how you *"survived in the wild"* (and maybe leave out the part where you drove into town for more marshmallows). Happy camping!

CHAPTER 20:
SURVIVING THE POLAR VORTEX
(AND OTHER LESSONS IN ENDURANCE)

Every few years, Wisconsin experiences a phenomenon so brutal, so bone-chilling, that it tests even the hardiest of Wisconsinites. I'm talking, of course, about the polar vortex—that Arctic blast that turns our state into a frozen tundra and makes even the most seasoned snow-shoveler reconsider their life choices. When the polar vortex hits, temperatures plummet, the wind bites with the ferocity of a rabid badger, and the entire state collectively agrees that it's just too darn cold.

But in true Wisconsin fashion, we don't just hunker down and wait for the polar vortex to pass—we find ways to make the best of it. After all, if you can survive a polar vortex, you can survive just about anything.

The Cold That Bites

The polar vortex is no ordinary cold snap. It's the kind of cold that makes your eyelashes freeze, your nose hairs turn to icicles, and your car battery give up in sheer defeat. It's the kind of cold that turns Lake Michigan into a giant slushy and turns your driveway into an ice rink. And when the wind chill hits negative 40 degrees, it's not just unpleasant—it's dangerous.

When the polar vortex descends upon Wisconsin, the entire state goes into survival mode. Schools close, businesses shut down, and everyone is advised to stay indoors unless absolutely necessary. But of course, there are always a few brave (or stubborn) souls who venture out, bundled up like human marshmallows, determined to prove that they can handle whatever Mother Nature throws at them.

One year, during a particularly brutal polar vortex, I decided to take a walk to the end of my driveway to check the mail. I bundled up in my heaviest coat, two pairs of gloves, and a scarf that covered everything except my eyes. The moment I stepped outside, the cold hit me like a punch to the face, and I immediately regretted my decision.

By the time I reached the mailbox, my eyelashes had frozen together, and I was seriously considering abandoning the mail and making a run for it. But I persevered, grabbed the stack of bills and catalogs, and hurried back to the house, my fingers numb and my pride slightly bruised.

When I got inside, my wife gave me a look that said, "Why on earth would you go out in this?"

"Had to check the mail," I replied, trying to sound casual.

"You're ridiculous," she said, shaking her head. "But at least you're dedicated."

The Joy of Staying Inside

One of the lessons every Wisconsinite learns during a polar vortex is the art of staying inside. When the temperatures drop below zero, and the wind chill makes it feel like you're living on the surface of Mars, there's no shame in curling up on the couch with a blanket, a cup of hot cocoa, and a good book. It's a time to embrace the Danish concept of "hygge"—the art of finding warmth and coziness in the midst of winter.

My family has a few traditions for surviving the polar vortex. For starters, there's "Soup Night," a weekly tradition where we make a big pot of soup or chili, crank up the heat, and settle in for a cozy evening. There's something comforting about the smell of simmering soup filling the house, the warmth of the fireplace, and the knowledge that outside, the world is frozen solid.

My personal favorite is my mom's beer cheese soup—a rich, creamy concoction made with sharp cheddar, a splash of local beer, and a whole lot of love. It's the kind of soup that warms you from the inside out, the perfect antidote to a cold Wisconsin winter.

"Stick to your ribs," my dad likes to say, ladling a generous portion into his bowl. "That's the secret to surviving the polar vortex."

Another essential part of polar vortex survival is finding ways to stay entertained indoors. For some, that means binge-watching their favorite TV shows or working on a jigsaw puzzle. For others, it's an excuse to dust off the old board games and challenge family members to a heated game of Monopoly or Scrabble.

In my house, we have a long-standing tradition of playing Euchre, a card game that's practically a religion in Wisconsin. My dad is a Euchre master, and he takes the game very seriously. He's been known to engage in some friendly trash talk, claiming that he can "read his opponents like a book." And while I'd like to say that I've inherited his skills, the truth is that I've lost more games of Euchre than I care to admit.

"Keep practicing, Wayne," my dad says with a grin. "One of these days, you'll beat me."

The Outdoor Die-Hards

Despite the brutal conditions, there are always a few outdoor die-hards who refuse to let a little thing like a polar vortex keep them inside. These are the folks who see subzero temperatures as a challenge, not a deterrent. They're the ones who go ice fishing in 30-below wind chills, hit the snowmobile trails in a blizzard, or take pride in being the first to shovel their driveway after a snowfall.

One year, during a particularly frigid polar vortex, my buddy Carl decided to go cross-country skiing at Blue Mound State Park. When I asked him if he was serious, he just shrugged and said, "Why not? It's good exercise."

"You know it's negative 20 degrees outside, right?" I replied, trying to sound reasonable.

"Just makes the workout more intense," Carl said, grinning. "Besides, I've got all the gear."

I wasn't about to join him, but I admired his determination. Carl came back from his skiing adventure with frost on his beard, a rosy glow in his cheeks, and a triumphant look on his face.

"Worth it," he declared, as if he'd just conquered Everest.

The Snow Shoveler's Workout

For many Wisconsinites, the polar vortex means one thing: snow shoveling. When the snow starts falling, there's no time to waste—you've got to get out there and clear the driveway before it turns into a sheet of ice. And while some folks rely on snowblowers to get the job done, there are plenty of die-hard shovelers who see it as a point of pride to clear their driveway the old-fashioned way.

My dad is one of those die-hard shovelers. He insists that shoveling is "good cardio" and claims that it builds character. And while I'm not sure if he's right about the character part, there's no denying that shoveling snow is a workout. It's a test of endurance, patience, and upper-body strength—especially when the snow is wet and heavy.

One winter, during a particularly bad polar vortex, my dad and I were out shoveling the driveway together. The wind was whipping snow into our faces, and the temperature was so low that the snow squeaked under our boots. We took turns shoveling, stopping every now and then to catch our breath and warm our fingers.

"This is brutal," I muttered, rubbing my hands together.

"Just think of it as nature's gym," my dad replied, grinning.

I wasn't sure if shoveling counted as a workout, but by the time we finished, I was sore, sweaty, and thoroughly exhausted. And as we stood there, admiring our work, my dad clapped me on the back and said, "You did good, Wayne. You've got the heart of a true Wisconsinite."

Embracing the Cold

For all its challenges, the polar vortex also brings out the best in Wisconsinites. It's a reminder that we're a resilient bunch, capable of finding humor, camaraderie, and even joy in the face of adversity. We know how to laugh at ourselves, how to find comfort in the little things, and how to appreciate the warmth of a hot drink, a cozy blanket, and a good book.

One year, during a particularly bad polar vortex, my wife and I decided to make the best of it by turning our living room into a makeshift cabin. We dragged the couch in front of the fireplace, piled on the blankets, and spent the weekend watching old movies, sipping hot toddies, and pretending we were snowed in at a cozy cabin in the Northwoods.

"See?" my wife said, smiling. "The polar vortex isn't so bad."

And she was right. In the end, it's all about perspective. The polar vortex might be cold and unforgiving, but it's also an opportunity to slow down, appreciate the warmth of home, and find joy in the little moments.

A Lesson in Resilience

Surviving the polar vortex isn't just about braving the cold—it's about embracing the challenges of winter and finding ways to make the best of it. It's about learning to laugh at the absurdity of frozen eyelashes, celebrating the small victories of shoveling a driveway, and finding comfort in the company of family and friends.

So the next time you find yourself facing a polar vortex, don't just hunker down and wait for it to pass. Embrace the cold, find the warmth in the little things, and remember that you're part of a long tradition of Wisconsinites who have faced the same challenges and come out stronger on the other side.

And if all else fails, just make a big pot of beer cheese soup and wait it out. Trust me—it works every time.

A Wisconsinite's Guide to Weather
Because in the Dairy State, Mother Nature likes to keep us guessing

The Four Seasons: Almost Winter, Winter, Still Winter, and Road Construction

In Wisconsin, the idea of traditional seasons is a mere suggestion. Instead, we experience:

- ❖ Almost Winter (September - November): When leaves change color, and everyone suddenly remembers that snow shovels exist.

- ❖ Winter (November - March... sometimes April): A frozen wonderland with occasional attempts by the sun to convince you to leave your house.

- ❖ Still Winter (March - May): When spring seems to arrive but is immediately followed by an April blizzard just to remind you who's boss.

- ❖ Road Construction (May - September): A magical time when all major highways are closed, and detours are your new best friend.

Dressing for Wisconsin Weather

The key to surviving Wisconsin weather is layers. You should be able to adapt from a -20°F wind chill to a sunny 65°F, all in a single day. Here's the basic formula:

- ❖ Base Layer: Long underwear, because once winter hits, your skin needs a hug.

- ❖ Mid-Layer: A hoodie (ideally Packers-themed) that says, "I'm cold, but I'm still proud."

- ❖ Outer Layer: A parka that can withstand a polar vortex, complete with a hood large enough to trap a small blizzard.

- ❖ Emergency Layer: A flannel jacket for the fall days when the wind is chilly, but the mosquitoes are still plotting revenge.

Snow: A Love-Hate Relationship

In Wisconsin, we don't just deal with snow; we embrace it. We have over a dozen words for snow, including:

❖ "Flurries": Light, whimsical snowflakes that make you think you can still wear tennis shoes.

❖ "Snow Showers": More serious, and definitely going to stick around longer than your cousin who "just dropped by."

❖ "Lake Effect Snow": When Lake Michigan decides to dump a few extra feet of snow just because it can.

❖ "Thundersnow": A phenomenon that makes you question all your life choices while simultaneously admiring nature's audacity.

Pro Tip: During the first snowfall of the season, everyone forgets how to drive. It's like a statewide amnesia event. If you're on the road, drive defensively and try not to laugh at the Illinois plates sliding into the ditch.

The Unpredictable Spring

Spring in Wisconsin is a practical joke. You'll get a few warm days in March, and just when you're ready to put away your winter coat, bam—you wake up to six inches of snow. Locals have a saying, "If you don't like the weather, wait five minutes," but really it's more like "If you think it's spring, don't get too comfortable."

Summer: Not Too Hot, Not Too Long

Summers in Wisconsin are glorious... and short. They're marked by barbecues, outdoor festivals, and everyone suddenly becoming an expert on mosquito repellents. However, don't let the sunny skies fool you—July and August can come with a side of surprise thunderstorms and humidity so thick, you could slice it and serve it with cheese.

Pro Tip: Always keep a rain jacket and sunscreen in your car. You might need both in the same afternoon.

Fall: The Tease Before Winter

Fall is arguably Wisconsin's best season. The leaves turn beautiful colors, and the temperatures are mild... until they're not. This is the season for pretending winter isn't just around the corner while enjoying pumpkin patches and tailgating like it's your job. But as soon as that first leaf falls, expect the following weather progression:

❖ Week 1: Crisp, cool air and sweater weather.

❖ Week 2: 70°F and sunny—people break out their shorts again.

❖ Week 3: Temperatures drop by 30 degrees overnight; flannel sales skyrocket.

❖ Week 4: Snow flurries appear, and everyone acts shocked, as if this wasn't inevitable.

The Polar Vortex

When meteorologists warn of a "polar vortex," what they really mean is, "Stay indoors unless you enjoy turning into a human popsicle." The polar vortex is a phenomenon that brings temperatures so low, the thermometer itself needs therapy. It's when Wisconsin tests your mettle and your antifreeze.

During this time:
- Pipes freeze.
- Cars refuse to start.
- Even the squirrels look annoyed.

The only upside? It's perfect weather for ice fishing and for proving you're tough enough to live in Wisconsin.

CHAPTER 21:
A LIFE WELL-LIVED IN WISCONSIN

As I sit here, putting the final touches on this collection of stories, I can't help but feel a deep sense of gratitude for the place I call home. Wisconsin, with its long winters, warm communities, and quirky traditions, has shaped me in more ways than I can count. It's a state that takes pride in its past, celebrates its present, and faces the future with a resilience that can only be forged in subzero temperatures.

When I started writing this book, my goal was simple: to share the stories and traditions that make Wisconsin special. I wanted to capture the essence of life in the Dairy State—the joy of a Friday night fish fry, the thrill of a Packers victory, the warmth of a campfire, and the humor of a tall tale told over a cold beer. But along the way, I realized that this book wasn't just about Wisconsin—it was about connection. Connection to the land, to the people, and to the shared experiences that bind us together.

The Spirit of Wisconsin

There's a spirit to this place that's hard to put into words. It's a combination of Midwestern friendliness, quiet resilience, and an unshakable belief that life is better when you've got a brat on the grill and a Leinenkugel's in hand. It's a state that knows how to laugh at itself, how to embrace the little moments, and how to find joy in the simple things.

I think back to all the stories I've shared—the legendary walleye that got away, the tractor pulls, the Polar Plunges, the Lambeau Leaps, and the endless supply of cheese curds—and I realize that these stories aren't just about what we do in Wisconsin. They're about who we are. We're a people who believe in hard work, but we also believe in having a good time. We know how to survive the cold, but we also know how to enjoy a summer day on the lake. We're proud of our traditions, but we're always ready to welcome a newcomer to the table.

A Place to Belong

Growing up in Wisconsin, I always felt a strong sense of belonging. There's something comforting about living in a place where everyone waves at you from their truck, where the local supper club knows your drink order, and where strangers at the grocery store strike up a conversation like you're old friends. It's a place where community matters, where people look out for each other, and where there's always an extra seat at the table.

Over the years, I've learned that Wisconsin isn't just a place to live—it's a place to belong. It's a place where the seasons mark the rhythm of life, where traditions are passed down with pride, and where the simplest things—a brat on the grill, a cold beer, or a quiet evening by the lake—can bring the greatest joy.

A Few Final Words of Advice

Before I wrap things up, I'd like to leave you with a few words of advice—lessons I've learned from a lifetime in the Great White Cheese State:

❖ Never say no to a Friday night fish fry. Trust me, you'll regret it.

❖ Always bring extra layers—you never know when the weather's going to turn.

❖ If you're at a tailgate, never put ketchup on your brat (unless you're prepared to defend your choices).

❖ Learn to polka. You don't have to be good at it, but you should at least give it a try.

❖ Respect the snow shoveler's code: clear your driveway, help your neighbor, and always wave at the plow driver.

❖ If you catch a big fish, go ahead and add a few inches to your story. It's a Wisconsin tradition.

❖ Never underestimate the power of a good cup of coffee, a warm bowl of soup, or a cold beer—especially when shared with good company.

❖ A Toast to the Good Life

As I bring this book to a close, I want to raise a virtual glass to all of you. Whether you're a born-and-raised Wisconsinite, a recent transplant, or just a curious reader looking to learn more about life in the Dairy State, I hope these stories have brought a smile to your face and a little warmth to your heart. I hope they've reminded you of the importance of finding joy in the simple things, of staying connected to your roots, and of embracing the quirks that make life interesting.

In Wisconsin, we have a saying that sums up our outlook on life: "Life is good on the water, and even better with good company." It's a reminder that the best moments aren't always the big ones—they're the quiet evenings on the lake, the laughter around the campfire, and the shared stories that bring us closer together.

So here's to Wisconsin: a state that knows how to laugh, how to celebrate, and how to endure. A state that's proud of its past, hopeful for its future, and always ready to welcome you with open arms and a plate of cheese curds. And here's to all of you, for taking this journey with me and for sharing in the spirit of the Great White Cheese State.

As we say in Wisconsin, "You betcha."

ABOUT THE AUTHOR

Wayne Larson was born and raised in the heart of Wisconsin, in a small town where the Friday night football games were as important as the Sunday church service, and the local supper club was the place to be. He grew up on a steady diet of bratwurst, cheese curds, and Packers victories, and has always been proud of his Midwestern roots.

A storyteller at heart, Wayne began his career as a journalist for the Pineville Press, where he covered everything from town hall meetings to the annual cranberry festival. Over the years, he's been a radio host, a fishing guide, and a volunteer firefighter—each role giving him new material for his ever-growing collection of tall tales and local legends.

When he's not writing, Wayne enjoys spending time outdoors, whether it's canoeing down the Wisconsin River, ice fishing on Lake Mendota, or grilling in his backyard (regardless of the weather). He's a self-proclaimed "supper club connoisseur" and takes pride in his ability to find the best fish fry within a 50-mile radius.

Wayne lives with his wife, Karen, who keeps him grounded and occasionally helps him fact-check his more outlandish stories. Together, they have two grown children who've inherited their father's love of the great outdoors and their mother's practicality.

Made in the USA
Middletown, DE
10 December 2024

66667485R00109